Our culture is in a very fluid time spiritually. While our traditional denominational structures continue to decline, the greatest emerging category for affiliation is the "nones." While conservative and strict religious groups continue to grow, more and more people describe themselves as "spiritual but not religious." While traditional theologies come more and more into question, still older wisdom emerges from centuries in the shadows.

As James Russell Lowell once wrote of another volatile time:

> Time makes ancient good uncouth,
> They must upward still and onward,
> Who would keep abreast of truth.

For any serious spiritual seeker, it can be an intimidating journey. And there is no better guide and companion for that journey than my friend the Rev. Dr. Jane Galloway. The inquiring mind and discipline of a scholar, the creative communicative skills of an artist but most importantly, the heart of a pastor, Jane shares with us not only the results of her academic study and years of experience in ministry but also the hard won learnings from her own journey. She does so in a way that is accessible and user friendly – producing for us, in her own words, a "tool box."

During our years as colleagues in ministry, I was always impressed by the clarity, intelligence, passion and compassion that Jane brought to her work as she sought to build a community of mutually supportive spiritual explorers. It is my hope that this work will inspire individuals to take their own journey and that as part of that journey, the need to be committed to and with others will be clear. Perhaps of all the many gifts of Jane's that I have learned to appreciate and admire, the one I cherish the most is that at the end of the day, she can't rest without seeking to get us connected to each other. Thank you Jane for your work and for this gift to help us on our way...

Peace and power to you,
REV. DR. ROBERT BRASHEAR NYC

I hear it all the time: people in recovery giving lip service to the spirituality of the 12 Steps – "I know this is a spiritual program!" – but never truly digging into what that means – beyond gaining some fluency and faith in a Higher Power. With *The Gateways: Wisdom of 12-Step Spirituality*, Galloway brings a much-needed burst of Interspiritual energy and insight to recovery as a *specifically* spiritual process, blending ritual, practice, body, and mind into a holistic model that provides real-world ways to work the steps within the context of spiritual living.

As we enter a New Era of consciousness and awakening, people in recovery will welcome this refreshing and highly energizing book for its far-reaching embrace of multiple paths. *The Gateways* into Perennial Truths shared by all wisdom traditions, resulting in a comprehensive approach to Spiritual Recovery. The *Big Book* has needed an infusion of deep and fresh spiritual energy and insight for a long while – and here it is!

JACK CUFFARI, INTERSPIRITUAL MINISTER

…let me tell you I find the way you marry the 12 Steps with the Spiritual to be just as important a concept as the *Big Book*. I feel as if you are talking directly to me in language that will especially appeal to modern society, especially women. I "hear" the Jane Galloway I know and have loved for so many years SHARING herself with me. I really believe that you have written an important work here. It's an enjoyable read and I find myself relating to it much more easily than I did to the Big Book the first time I read that.

You my dear, are RIGHT on target, and RIGHT on time. You are on the cutting edge of a new revolution in the field of alcohol and addiction answers. I feel SO amazingly grateful to be a part of this. Your book is really helping me in my own sobriety and in my Spiritual Path. I finally have a Spiritual Path. That's what's been missing for my entire Sobriety.

JUDITH LONIAK L.V.N.

Bill W., Lois, and Dr. Bob are cheering from the bleachers as Jane Galloway brings the much-beloved 12 Steps of Alcoholics Anonymous into the light of the 21st century. Touching upon all the world's religious traditions, as well as secular and New Thought philosophies, *The Gateways* serves as a guide to anyone on a spiritual journey who wants to deepen their faith and experience what it means to be made whole. Jane Galloway knows what it's like to hit rock bottom, and thanks to the spiritual practices she's developed in over thirty-five years of working the Steps one day at a time, we can also know, along with her, the kind of recovery that soars high above the clouds.

KATE SHEEHAN ROACH
MANAGING EDITOR, PATHEOS SPIRITUALITY

THE GATEWAYS

THE WISDOM OF 12-STEP SPIRITUALITY

Dynamic Practices That Work

Jane S. Galloway

Sacred Stories
PUBLISHING

Books may be purchased through booksellers or by contacting Sacred Stories Publishing.

The Gateways: The Wisdom of 12-Step Spirituality
Jane S. Galloway
Tradepaper ISBN: 978-1-945026-17-1
Electronic ISBN: 978-1-945026-18-8
Library of Congress Control Number: 2016945717

Cover Concepts and Illustrations by Caitlin Crest ~ ZephyrGraphics.com
Interior Design by Casey Hooper ~ cpaperie.com

Published by Sacred Stories Publishing, LLC
Delray Beach, FL
www.sacredstoriespublishing.com

Printed in the United States of America

I grew up in a sea of conversations about alcohol, but where no one drank, with people whose lives had all been impacted by the negative effects of the drug.

My dad was in AA, an active, charismatic, excited member, who spoke to early conventions and worked with others from two years before my birth until his death from smoking when I was sixteen. My maternal grandmother was a lifetime member of the Woman's Christian Temperance Union, and her family had endured tragedy in Ireland for generations because of alcohol.

I watched my dad change from a newly sober person with anger issues, into a spiritual seeker, someone who won the top award for sales in his international company, stood on his head every day, introduced me to metaphysics, astrology, Dale Carnegie's *How to Win Friends and Influence People*, *The Complete Works* of Sigmund Freud, and *The Prophet* by Kahlil Gibran, all before I was sixteen.

I saw sobriety work. I had no clue I would end up hitting my own bottom and becoming a 12-Step person, but once I figured it out, my role model for a sober life was my dad…and he was a movie star to me.

One of the last things he shared with me before he left the planet was his understanding about God. We were in Colorado on vacation, and he showed me a book by Emmett Fox, the *Little Red Book* of AA and *The Prophet* by Kahlil Gibran.

One month later he had a heart attack, and even though he had been advised not to do his yoga in the hospital, he insisted and probably that headstand was not a great idea. But really, what a way to go.

Thank you Daddy. Eddie Galloway, I love you. YOU GAVE ME LIFE, AND YOU SHOWED ME A WAY TO LIVE IT.

I hope this book pays the gift forward and makes you proud, wherever you are doing headstands these days.

Love, Janie

This book is dedicated to Edna Jane Brown Stormont, my grandmother and best friend. Thank you Grandma, for seeing me, truly seeing me, for praying for me every day, and for teaching me about God. I know each of your prayers got through. Thank you, bless you. I love you.

It is also dedicated to Art Lockard, Sheila Savage, and Maureen Lee, each of whom was there waiting for me at the other side of the bottom that thrust me into this 12-Step world. Your love made all the difference, and your dedication to the Steps, to the process of recovery, and to a spiritual solution were the miracle that brought me into the light.

And finally to Mike Patchett, who never stops believing in me, no matter what.

THE 12 STEPS – A WAY INWARD

"Nothing that is human is alien to me."

-PLAYWRIGHT TENNESSEE WILLIAMS

"In our language there is no word to say inferior or superiority or equality because we are equal; it's a known fact. But life has become very complicated since the newcomers came here. And how does your spirit react to it? It's painful. You have to be strong to walk through the storm. I know I'm a bridge between two worlds. All I ask is for people to wash their feet before they try to walk on me."

-ALANIS OBOMSAWIN, ABENAKI

"For native people who speak their language, English can be very confusing. Many times you cannot express in English the true meaning of Indian words. When we hear something in English we sometimes react or our spirit reacts. Sometimes we need to use English words out of order to express our true meanings. We need to be patient and pray. Living in two worlds can be difficult. Life is painful sometimes. The pain of life is where the lessons are learned."

WISDOM OF NATIVE AMERICAN ELDERS

CONTENTS

FOREWORD: ARE YOU READY FOR A CHANGE?
REV. DR. CECIL L. "CHIP" MURRAY

This is no small change, for you can't nickel and dime this author who is personal witness to the God who can make the metaphysical physical, and the physical metaphysical. Dr. Jane Stormont Galloway takes you from bottom to top, daring you to first hit the bottom, and then to experience the Jesus path that takes you to the top. There you come to see that the bottom can be your breakthrough . . . or your breakdown, the decision being made by you from the inside.

Significant people in our lives help us choose the positive, people like the grandmother to whom "Stormy" dedicates the book, door openers for wounded warriors who are challenged to sink or swim.

The author invites us to fear not the bottom, but to dare to reach for the mountaintop without losing our minds. We know that thousands of people climb Mt. Everest each year since Tenzing and Lord Hilary broached the top. So far eight of these have died this year from exhaustion, not from reaching for the top, but from descending to the bottom.

The 12-Step Program is the pathway, originating in the middle of the 20th century to emerge as the prototypical Alcoholics Anonymous. The essence is that the pursuit of truth is the greatest journey; so the writer does not attempt to remove the 12-Step Program, but to stabilize it. That is, far too many of us are rescued from the bottom only to relapse once we reach the top. Tracing baby boomers through their life stages indicates the thirst for fullness via the 12-Step Program...the thirst is quenched by the next stage and new component of teaching, "Do not give up. Give in."

Stormy understands that preparation for the *whole* journey requires *whole* and *holistic* preparation, so she makes full and extensive introduction to the GATEWAY concept before the gate. She gives breadth of scope, drawing from such as the Nag Hammadi scrolls and the different *ism's* of the faith-based systems, alerting the majority of "I'm spiritual, but not religious" believers to see that the author is transcending standard religious approaches by giving us a new gospel. She is in the category of the designer of "Summa Metaphysica," David Birnbaum, who with book one, "God and Evil," and book two, "God and Good," gives us the next and greatest challenge of the 21st century: *Q4PQuest For Potential* — how the very essence of God, of the cosmos, and of every living creature is striving to reach its own excellence.

The Gateways are a pathway for the inward journey, on which the 12-Steps are a key to the rediscovery of the Jesus Path via spirituality, not religion. The Gateways open the way even for those who have not experienced the original 12-Step Program for alcoholism. Each Gateway starts with a question:

Do you want to be healed?
Are you prepared to endure the inner journey?

If Yes, then let's go, remembering that the journey starts within. Buckle your seat belt for the ride of a lifetime!

Rev. Dr. Cecil "Chip" Murray joined the faculty of USC after retiring from his post as pastor of First African Methodist Episcopal Church (FAME) Los Angeles, CA. Dr. Murray was appointed as the John R. Tansey Chair of Christian Ethics in the School of Religion at the University of Southern California, and in addition, was named a senior fellow of the Center for Religion and Civic Culture. He chairs the USC Cecil Murray Center for Community Engagement. Murray holds a doctorate from Claremont School of Theology and has many years of experience as a senior statesman in the African American community and in the city of Los Angeles as a whole.

INTRODUCTION: WHY 12-STEP SPIRITUALITY?

The 12-Steps of Alcoholics Anonymous are an authentic spiritual path. They are an organic, developmental healing process, a series of inner moves, first discovered by a group of hopeless drunks in mid 20th Century United States, who became the founders of Alcoholics Anonymous. They have evolved to become a part of a much larger cultural/spiritual shift, and have birthed a kind of 12-Step Nation.

AA is also a spiritual recovery program and the 12-Steps are how it works. The good news is that there is nothing religious about the spiritual part of this program. The basic idea is to admit that you are not single-handedly running the Universe, and to turn your messed up, addicted, worn out life over to the power that makes the trees grow and holds the planets in the sky. Whatever that power is doing, it is doing a better job of it than anyone crawling in the door of their first 12-Step meeting. That is really it! Turning our lives over to the care of a power

greater than ourselves is the key to entering the spiritual path of the 12-Steps.

The 12-Step Path immediately confronts us with a seeming paradox – "Surrender to win."

All wisdom teachings contain paradox. Like the Zen Koan, "what is the sound of one hand clapping?," a paradox is a statement that seems on the surface to contradict itself, but with further contemplation opens to a deeper knowing.

The 12-Steps are called a bridge back to life, but too often we find ourselves hanging out on the bridge with other recovering people because "life" as it currently exists isn't a place we really want to fit in. What I am proposing is not just a change in the way we approach our personal spirituality, but also a culture change. We live in a global age, and the universal tongue is the language of the heart. But we don't have a universal spiritual language. The 12-Steps are potentially that language, for the millions of people worldwide who are interested in a planet where we celebrate oneness, spirituality, and holistic healing in community.

The goal of 12-Step Spirituality is to create conditions through which as many people can connect to Source as possible. The Steps are a support system that "props us up on every leaning side," but one that doesn't limit God. The goal of working them is to open you to the power and the Presence, and to create a way for the unlimited potential in you to actualize. And frankly, God will take care of the rest.

After years of trying to share my own spiritual walk with the 12-Steps through AA meetings and sponsorship, ordained ministry, public speaking and teaching, I finally got it that no one can have a spiritual awakening for anyone else. Trust me on this. I have tried.

Some people call it evangelism, others call it motivational speaking, or even codependence, but that's another book. If what theologian John Wesley said were really true; that the way to convert people was to "catch on fire and others will love to come and watch you burn," I would have set many buildings and people on fire by now. I have *been* on fire, and also been a catalyst for change in many people, but coercing people to join anything is not my style. It isn't the deeper truth of the 12-Step Path either, as it works through "attraction – not promotion."

I have always shared my experience, strength and hope freely, but I'm very clear that the magic of those moments has had to do with a kind of alchemy of readiness and timing, the student being ready and the teacher appearing. I do know something about staying the course. I have followed a path of sobriety and spiritual evolution for many years now, by working 12-Steps over and over, deeper and deeper, year after year, adding different tools and practices along the spiral path inward, but always supported by the Twelve Steps, and in so doing have discovered realms beyond my own imagining.

I have also had a lot of fun, met fabulous people, traveled the world, had amazing personal and professional experiences, suffered great loss and had unbelievable good fortune, and continue to live life as part of a marvelous international fellowship of the Spirit. It has seemed to me for a long time that the principles and practices of the 12-Steps could work for many people who aren't addicted if they were explained well enough as a universal path. I have heard countless self-help gurus and ministers try to do this, but unfortunately these interpretations often promise something I call "12-Steps Lite," a self-interested, quasi spiritual, self-help pseudo psychological version of the Steps, minus the key component of selfless service.

But, personal transformation through the 12-Steps *depends* upon a life of service. There is no "there there" without it. Actually, freeing us from a narcissistic focus on ourselves is the whole point of the 12-Steps! Sharing the gift is what changes everything and keeps the spiral of growth going. You can't keep it unless you give it away, is one way to say it. Another paradox. In any case, a pseudo version just doesn't work, and the Steps are nothing if they aren't practical. They work, and people who need the Steps, need them to work. Our lives depend upon it.

Addicted people definitely aren't the only ones who go through dark nights of the soul. We *all* need support, and if I may be so bold, our world would be a lot better off if we decided to share the wealth with one another. A spiritual path like the one created by the 12-Steps is a great addition to our world.

Truth is universal, and comes from the Source of all creation, whatever we call it/her/him. This is actually a good description of the 12-Step Path as well. The spiritual path of the Steps cuts out the middleman of any organized religion, and offers a system to get back in sync with our animating force, in community. It is not a religion, but the program is spiritual, and the goal of working the Steps is to become sane and sober and productive, and to be of service.

THE WISDOM PATH

It was at a conference at the Seed Graduate Institute in New Mexico, where quantum physicists and Native American Medicine elders met to discuss and ceremonially affirm their common understanding of the web (Chief Seattle), the quantum field (Albert Einstein) and other esoteric truths, that I met theoretical quantum physicist Dr. Amit Goswami (What The Bleep). I approached him after his astonishing lecture and asked him what path he personally follows. He answered simply "The Wisdom Path."

The Wisdom Path runs through all great traditions, but is not any of those paths. It is where science and spirituality coexist. It is a river of Truth that is timeless, and has been the source of inspiration for writers, philosophers, poets, artists and mystics for time immemorial. The Wisdom Path is the muse, the living Spirit, the Well of Living Waters. The Wisdom Path is the spirituality of the 12-Steps.

Wisdom teachings can be understood on different levels but each path leads to the same place. Matthew Fox describes it perfectly with the title of his book about the wisdom path, "One River, Many Wells." The wells represent different religions: Christianity, Buddhism, Islam, Judaism, Shinto, Zoroastrianism etc. Each of the wells is distinct, but they all are methods to reach water. The river represents the Source of all creation, upon which they all draw. It is communion with the RIVER that we seek.

The 12-Steps *begin* at the river and go deeper. The Gateways are that well into a progressive, inter-spiritual, practical 12-Step spirituality for people who are hungry for a path beyond religion. It works. Did I say that before? I'll say it again. It works, and too many people relapse because they can't find a spiritual path that works for them.

The 12-Steps create a scaffolding to support and contain a life of spiritual growth. They are practical, and in theological language, are a humanistic, holistic, systematic theology. The path may be too rigorous for those who are not desperate, but maybe it hasn't been explained well enough as a system that isn't about just addiction. I am always hoping that just one more stab at the thing may open a door for someone. Call me crazy, but hope springs eternal.

Here are some of the questions I have asked myself along this road:

1. Is it possible that the rigors and discipline of the 12-Step Path are simply too great for anyone but the truly lost to latch onto?
2. Can recovering people mainstream successfully into an addicted society?
3. Where do we go from this place of newly found sobriety and health, and a Utopian practice of rigorous self-honesty, to avoid slipping back into old, unhealthy habits?
4. Is there a way to move the conversation about 12-Step Spirituality beyond the addiction and recovery model for individuals, and into a wider spiritual movement for a pluralistic society?

I expressed these questions, along with a lot of other frustrations, to a friend, who told me that I needed to write down what works for me as a spiritual path, and that in so doing, I would be offering a great tool for people both in and out of recovery who are willing to seek.

I am nothing if not willing.

What works for me is the 12-Steps of AA, lived and practiced as a spiral path going deeper. Along the way, and in addition to practicing the Steps in community, I have benefitted from many teachings, primarily the Jesus Path and the Nag Hammadi Scrolls, along with many spiritual practices and ways of living that contribute to an ever-evolving inner awakening. The 12-Steps are the constant, the framework, the beginning and really the end. I also do like a lot of other people in recovery do: I walk a path that calls for honesty, open mindedness, regular inner house cleaning and willingness, humility and selfless service, and I have done so with great dedication for many years. Honestly, we do this because we need to, in order to save our own lives each day. And it turns out to be way easier than hustling constantly too.

After early recovery, when we are feeling better and into the flow of things, we want to be about the game of life and many recovering people become very successful in professional and civic endeavors. But in the area of spirituality, things seem to be a little more complicated. A lot of us try to return to organized religion, but discover that there is often too much untreated addiction and codependence in churches. Talk about irony! In my years of pastoral ministry I discovered, to my surprise, that many people actually attend church to avoid hitting bottom with one addiction or another. That is definitely not a place for sober people to hang out. So I guess I am trying to change church from a social club into a place where people are passionate about their spiritual walk. Here is the paradox: the entry place for the 12-Step spiritual path is actually *at* rock bottom, that place most of us spend years trying to avoid. I sure did!

But when I finally dropped the boulder I was carrying, of unprocessed grief and trauma, alcohol and drug addiction, I discovered there was a trampoline waiting for me that bounced me upward into a new stratosphere, where I met my future self! Hitting bottom was my scariest moment and my greatest gift; the end of one life and the beginning of another, and it can be for you too.

Remember, pain is part of life, but suffering is largely optional. Here's another paradox: if we insist upon denying pain or covering it up – which is what addiction is all about – we will simply prolong our suffering and will also miss the gift of the bounce, the rebirth, the conversion, the quantum jump forward. So by allowing the pain to be heard, we heal.

Another paradox: becoming "weller than well" is one of the outcomes of walking the 12-Step Path. This counter-cultural walk, based on telling the truth, and being of service eliminates a lot of the fat and cuts to the chase. It's ironic really, that recovering people, who have once been so out of control, can discover themselves out of step for a whole other reason, an outsider still.

So here it is: a companion guide for 12-Step spirituality, that uses as the central scaffolding of the inner journey, the Steps. Accompanying each Step are many tools that can be used to deepen the spiritual journey. Remember, this is not designed to replace the recovery component of the 12-Steps. It is really a way of integrating a practical spirituality into the process of the Steps, and as a resource for lifelong Step-11 work.

Step Eleven – *Sought through prayer and meditation to improve our conscious contact with God as we understand God, praying only for knowledge of God's will for us, and the power to carry it out.*

To support this path, I have created the Gateways, a kind of toolbox and guide for the 12-Step journey, a Technicolor spiritual system to accompany the 12-Steps, for beginners and old timers, for recovering addicts and people who aren't addicted, for seekers and folks who need a boost or a new idea at a down moment.

Each Gateway incorporates basic step work, along with a spiritual teaching, a Chakra or a Stage from Maslow's Hierarchy of Needs, a Concept, Color, Sacred Geometric Shape, Emotional component, Meridian, Gland, Musical Note or vibration, gemstone and several experiential rituals for working each level.

Accompanying the Gateways, is a Trans-cultural, Inter-spiritual Bento Box of tools that any seeker can draw upon. Like the selections in Japanese lunch boxes, many combinations can work. The 12-Steps are the consistent component, the box, if you will.

The Gateways are a bridge for people, in and outside of the recovery rooms, to find a way into the inner way through the 12-Steps. It can be used in community, as part of a church program, or as a way to practice a daily spiritual walk.

My hope is that something in these pages will be the spark that opens a door inward for you, and that once that door has opened, you will enter and "know a new freedom and a new happiness" and will… "be amazed before you are half-way through." (AA, pages 83-84 –The Promises)

Enjoy the journey inward. Your discoveries along the way will add to mine, and will be the key to someone else's liberation, so pass on anything that works for you. That's how this thing works. And we will surely meet one another on "the road to happy destiny."

~Jane

{ hope }

MY STORY

The first time I went to an AA meeting I was beaten, out of good ideas, sad, lost and physically and emotionally sick. Even though I was still working in the New York theatre, appearing on television regularly, and even occasionally on the famous Page Six gossip column of the New York Post, I knew that I was on the way down, into a deep abyss of despair and addiction.

I simply could not stop drinking, and using stimulant drugs to keep me going. I initially used amphetamine diet pills to control my weight, and I worked in an industry where being thin was a ticket to work. But the side effect of the diet pills was that I also didn't feel psychological pain as long as I could keep from coming down, and that was worth figuring out. I was afraid to face the pain under the addiction, so I just kept going and going until I broke.

I believed in God from childhood and was raised in the Presbyterian Church. I was actually a Presbyterian minister's stepdaughter, sang in the choir, and joined the church of my own free will in my early teens.

And then, my world collapsed. My father died from a heart attack, my minister stepfather left ministry and our family just one year later, and my life went into an emotional free fall. Within two years, I simply decided not to believe in a God who would abandon good people this way.

Most addicted people are hypersensitive, very creative, have higher than average intelligence and seek out a substance or behavior to manage pain. That pain is often rooted in childhood. I also had a traumatic childhood. Some of you may relate.

Trauma structurally changes our brains, hurts our hearts, and our ability to navigate the world. I thought from an early age that these traumas had impacted me organically, I could literally feel it in my brain, but it wasn't until recently that medical science began to confirm this. What a relief! If it is something organic that is broken, there is also a way to fix it.

I also come from a family of people historically impacted by addiction to alcohol. Alcoholism is a very tricky syndrome that affects not only the person who is addicted, but also the entire family system. Some call it a disease, others a constellation of behaviors and allergies. Whatever you call it, the presence of addiction in a family creates an environment where people dance around "the elephant in the living room," guessing at "normal," repressing anger, sadness, rage and anxiety, trying to control one another's behaviors, and generally feeling like something is very wrong but not being able to speak about it. Some of the untreated family system rules are "Don't Talk, Don't Trust, Don't Feel," and dysfunctional communication patterns are passed down through generations. These behaviors constitute the "ism" of alcoholism, and one can have the "ism" without ever taking a drink or drug.

Honestly my parents, all three of them, were great people. They all loved me to the best of their abilities, and I know they wanted to give me a great life. As a couple my mother and father were combustible. Their marriage came to a dramatic end when I was only 18 months old, after I verbally intervened in a fight between them. I was hyper vigilant and on red alert way too early. My stepfather was an engaged stepparent, a loving and clueless young man when he stepped into the role of co-parenting me when I was six years old and he was in his late twenties. His parenting deeply shaped my social conscience and as I have witnessed the mess many "blended families" make of this now common form of family, I am amazed at the relative sanity and maturity of all three of my parents in forging into that territory without a roadmap. But a lot of traumatic stuff happened in spite of all their good intentions, and I was damaged in the process.

My stepfather actually made a very direct and unsolicited amend to me when I was in my thirties. He apologized for my having been "the hockey puck in a lot of people's power games." He said he was truly sorry for his part in that. It was an amazingly healing moment actually. While I sort of hated hearing that it really had been as bad as I remembered, there is a releasing power in the act of making amends. I have never had one made to me other than this one from my stepfather, and it honestly healed something in me that had hurt for a long time. Jesus was right. The truth really does set you free.

It is likely that my brain was already operating from a "fight or flight" perspective when I was born. My mother was unhappy in her marriage to my father and during her pregnancy with me, so anxiety and sadness were the chemicals bathing my developing nervous system in utero. And as I have already mentioned, I was also naturally predisposed to addiction. There was alcoholism on both sides of my family for generations, along with untreated grief, codependency, food issues and other compulsive behaviors, but the untreated traumatic experiences of my early life made it even more likely that I would seek some chemical relief. If the trauma had been treated soon after it happened, who knows if I would have needed to self-medicate, but that didn't happen. People who moralize about addictions don't understand that addiction is pain control. Becoming addicted is the unfortunate by-product of what begins as a great self-help survival tool.

We also arrest emotional development at the age when we pick up our first addictive substance. In my case that was when I was sixteen, and for at least ten years, my emotional self was pretty much stuck there. But we don't stop living. Instead we develop a personality that is shaped by addiction, social norms and fear of rejection, and all of this is kept in a kind of suspended reality by using whatever substance or behavior or both, keep us from feeling the pain we are trying to avoid.

The problem with self-prescribed and administered drug therapy is that our bodies develop tolerance to these substances, and we need more and more of the substance to get the same result. Eventually the medication becomes the problem, years of buried pain can't be suppressed any more, and if we are lucky, we hit bottom and seek treatment.

So-called process addictions mirror the phenomenon of developing tolerance as well. Codependency, gambling, shopping, sex and repetitive action addictions release the same brain chemicals that substance addicts release by using a drug or alcohol or food. It is all about hormones. What happens with process addiction that is different from substance abuse is that we can only scare, excite or romance ourselves into a heightened state so many times before we simply wear out our adrenal glands. Producing fight or flight doses of adrenaline is only meant to give us a jolt of energy occasionally when we are in real danger, like running away from a tiger or lifting a car off of somebody. When we manufacture these stress hormones habitually, as many codependents do, eventually our body just says no.

I hit my bottom one night very late. My first love had just told me he was marrying someone else. It wasn't like he just made this decision without trying to engage me in some meaningful conversation about how our relationship might work. He did. He tried hard. But I was unable to show up for that conversation. I now know that we were not the right life match, and maybe I even knew that then but I wasn't ready to face it. This particular Monday evening, he came over for dinner, as he did many Monday evenings, but this time, he told me he was getting married.

I went into shock. I started talking really fast and I can't really remember how I made it through the rest of the evening. I do know that copious amounts of scotch were involved.

He left my apartment, and I was stone cold sober, in spite of having drunk half a fifth of scotch. This is an awful hell beyond words, and is just one of the symptoms of developing tolerance. In the stillness of my Greenwich Village apartment, I experienced an existential void and true despair beyond description. In that moment I "saw" myself at the center of a circle of isolation that I had created. I had pushed everyone I knew cared for me out of my life, and I had one horrible, timeless moment of living hell. It is hard to fully describe, but it was a moment of the deepest despair, depression, physical drunkenness and existential emptiness I had ever experienced or ever wish to experience again. I was utterly alone in the Universe.

At that moment a brilliant white light came into the room, and a voice came with it. I know Light isn't supposed to talk but this one actually did. I was lying in bed, pretending to read a book, sipping expensive brandy, and free falling into the void. And then time stopped. The room was suffused with a bright white light, a peaceful hum, and this white talking light said, "It's over. It's the drinking."

And it was. It was over, thank God. This moment was what I think is meant by Grace. Something came to get me from the pit of despair, and the next day I began a whole other life. Well, I was actually sick as a dog and hung over, and THEN I started a whole new life.

I attended my first 12-Step meeting that day and told the people at the meeting about the Light. To my great surprise I looked out at a room of people nodding their heads in recognition. It was amazing. They knew what I was talking about. I guess maybe some version of the Light came to get them too.

Something else happened at that meeting. I was sitting quietly, all dressed up and sure no one could tell I was an alcoholic. I laugh at this now, but we clutch onto our illusions until the last second. I was literally inhaling the meeting. I could not hear enough about these people's experiences. I saw myself in every one of their stories. Toward the end of the meeting, the leader looked right at me and said, "Young lady, would you like to share with us?" I couldn't believe it. Just to show you how crazy I really was, the thought that went through my mind was "Oh they probably think I am from the New York Times and writing a story about AA."

Huh? Out of touch you say? Grandiose? Just a bit. But the deeper part of me knew that if I did not get up and walk to the front of that small basement room and speak, I could not guarantee that I would ever go back. I knew that it was a matter of life and death.

When I got to the front of the room, my mouth began to move and I said, "My name is Jane, and I am an alcoholic." The second I said that my entire life to date literally flashed before my eyes. I can't explain it. This was an amazing experience, and I am sure it lasted only a couple of seconds in real time. I was experiencing a death and reincarnation on this plane. I felt it happen! My name was the same, my Social Security number is the same, but my essence evolved forward in that moment. I had entered another lifetime.

For at least a year all I did was try to get better. I worked really, really hard on my program, grieved the loss of my father in my early teens, and the divorce of my mother and stepfather two years later, both losses I had never fully let myself feel. My body went through a major purge after ninety days, beginning with a high fever and bronchial inflammation that then raged through my entire body. I was purging from both ends and every orifice, and crying and sobbing at the same time. That was kind of scary, and I think some people do this purge more gradually, but I later read about the exact process in a book on Zen healing. I wish I had read that book sooner, because it suggested that if we purge this way, when it is over we will crave some of the things we have let go of, and if we don't take them back into our bodies we will lose the craving for them. I had already had a hot fudge sundae and a big steak by that time. Oh well. I did let go of a two pack a day smoking habit after that illness though.

After a few months of going to meetings and detoxing, while appearing eight times a week in a popular Off Broadway play, I began an inventory and shared it all with my sponsor, Sheila. I made lists, made amends, prayed my head off and went to a lot of meetings. And slowly but surely I got better.

The talking Light transformed me in the blink of an eye, but I needed to take the steps to catch up to the new me. I can't believe I resisted hitting bottom for so long. I never want to go back there, and that bottom was my greatest gift. If I ever think I might like to have a vodka martini with olives in the lobby of the Plaza Hotel, all I have to do is remember that I didn't hit bottom at the Plaza…not by a long shot.

So that's my story! One night, in the depth of my despair, a talking light came into the room, and my life changed forever, one day at a time. If you are struggling with addiction, or are trying to stay clean, or with depression or trauma or despair and are wondering how you will ever make it, I can tell you. When you are at your darkest moment the forces for good in the Universe, the Source of all creation, the Light, Allah, God, Harry, whatever you call it, will rush to your aid if you ask. I wish this for you from the depth of my being.

The great news is that we are successfully intervening on these painful patterns much earlier than at anytime in history, and there is truly hope for breaking generational patterns of pain and creating a new life of possibilities earlier. Your bottom doesn't have to be like mine. Yours might be a lot lighter or heavier, but the moment of entry into this 12-Step way of life and the Promises is through the doorway of the bottom that is the end for you. I have experienced the miracle of living two lives in one lifetime, and you can too, one day at a time. The Realm of Spirit *is* broad, roomy, all-inclusive and ever present, as the 12-Step literature suggests.

Welcome to the first day of the rest of your life.

{ peace }

A SPIRITUAL HUNGER

AA literature suggests that beyond pain control, alcoholism is "a low level search for God," a short-term fix for a deeper hunger. The 12-Steps open us to a path along which that search can take place. This is a path that is non-judgmental, practical, and progressive; that goes both deep and wide, and when practiced, becomes a way of life. Growing up with a fair amount of chaos in my life, I took to the simple wisdom, order and stability of the Steps like a fish to water. The Steps were like oxygen for me. I felt like I could finally breathe for the first time.

Spiritual healing from addictions and family system wounding is a process. Think of yourself as a tree that has put down roots. The trunk is your essential self, the shallower roots are the family system for this incarnation and the deeper roots connect to the ancestors. Now think of the deep rich soil as your Source, as God, Great Spirit or whatever you call the animating power that breathes you. 12-Step Recovery connects us through our root system to the Source of all creation and the strong tree that flourishes as a result is our true self.

Addiction begins to develop when we can't face the pain of something. We just don't want to feel it, or fear that we can't feel it without breaking, so we find a way to go on with chemical help. And that help numbs us well enough so that we can keep going for a bit. But the self we develop under those conditions isn't connected to our true *essence*. It can't be! We will be making decisions about core issues, who to love and how to live, under the influence of fear and some mood altering substance or behavior. On top of that, we are also usually trying to please everybody in the world too.

Our soul always knows who we are though. We just need to remember. The journey of the first phase of recovery is about finding our way back to "God." We are always homesick until we do.

{ *think* }

A COUNTRY SPIRALS INTO ADDICTION

AA began in 1935 in Akron Ohio, but it really began to grow after WW II, when thousands of veterans returned home from the war, a patriotic effort that had mobilized a majority of the American populace. Some women worked in defense plants as riveters and administrative support, families saved scraps of aluminum foil and "made do" with margarine dyed with yellow food coloring pellets to save on use of dairy products that were needed for the war effort, and people "did without" to support this effort. When it was over, people were more than ready to stop sacrificing.

A big public relations effort went into selling a new consumer society to the returning GI's. Along with a focused effort to free up manufacturing jobs for the returning men, and the GI Bill that created opportunities for affordable individual home ownership for thousands of returning vets, the nuclear family ideal became the new norm, and the extended family support system, that had worked for thousands of years, became old hat. This was a short-term social experiment that ended up having disastrous results.

This social shift changed many women's roles from members of a multi-generational family support network to isolated "perfect" housewives and stay at home moms. Rosie the Riveter had to make a fast costume change into the suburban housewife, and very early in this social experiment, doctors began prescribing "mother's little helpers"- tranquilizers and amphetamines, to numb the symptoms of this new isolated role. Drinking at home during the day was added to this chemical bath to manage isolation, role stress, boredom, and loneliness.

Meantime, the husbands were drinking two martini lunches; kids were living in a world of the new processed foods, the family dinner table was replaced by TV dinners, and all of this in the name of PROGRESS! Even if families were not squeezing themselves into this crazy perfect nuclear family ideal, they were aspiring to it.

Advertisers splashed "The American Dream" all over the place. A house with a white picket fence, two cars, three kids, a perky happy smiling Stepford wife and a suit wearing breadwinning father, became the playbook. The economy was good, whatever that meant, and after a long traumatic war, the thought of unending prosperity was a relief on the surface. At least that is what people *thought* they thought.

But the new ideal started breaking almost as soon as it was implemented. Without extended family support, nuclear families came under too much pressure and the divorce rate began to escalate. Even young children suffered from migraine headaches and all manner of stress related illness. The pharmaceutical industry replaced the art of medicine and the human touch. Mental illness and neurosis in general also skyrocketed, as the most sensitive among us lost the support of a community safety net to keep them connected.

I am not suggesting that the old way was perfect. It was not. Alcoholism had been a huge public health problem, and after Prohibition became an even larger epidemic. Families were devastated by a father's pressure release if it came in the form of drinking, and poverty, child labor, domestic violence and sweatshops caused misery for thousands of Americans. But it is possible to try to fix something by over correcting, and this cultural movement after WW ll is an example of that.

Of course, this suburban dream was largely designed for white people, who moved out of the cities en-masse, into property insulated from integration by state and federal laws to prohibit selling to black families. But even so, the American Dream ideal snuck its way into everyone's subconscious mind, white, black, brown, immigrant, wealthy and poor, and "progress" became the deeper obsession of a nation.

Consumerism was our new national religion, shopping the spiritual practice, shopping malls the mecca and meeting place, substance abuse the fuel, patriotism and The American Dream, the cultural playbook. The Price Is Right was the name of the game, and seemingly everybody could be bought.

HOW DID THIS HAPPEN?

You have heard of Sigmund Freud. But did you know about his nephew Edward Bernays? Probably not, unless you know the history of advertising. Mr. Bernays is known as "the Father of Public Relations," a title he won by using his uncle's work on the subconscious mind to develop propaganda for the U.S. government ("Making the world safe for democracy"), and a method for advertisers on "Madison Avenue" to become the silent persuaders of a nation, and later a world. Bernays believed that it was important to harness the crowd or herd instinct in human beings, through unconscious suggestion. After he successfully marketed the First World War as "making the world safe for democracy," he commented publicly that, "if the American people will buy that, they will fall for anything."

The power of suggestion, Advertising Age

Weekly, Dale Carnegie's *How to Win Friends and Influence People* all became drivers of the new national ethic of Progress, and the American Dream ideal was planted into the minds of anyone who could read, see, hear or knew somebody who could, in post WW ll America. First radio and then the new medium of television were propaganda machines disguised as entertainment, selling a new family ideal and the lifestyle to go along with it. Actually radio and TV were designed to sell products! William Paley, CEO of CBS, developed the idea of soap operas to break up advertising for soap and cigars on CBS radio. Soap and cigars were the point. The entertainment kept people tuning in.

Television shows like *Ozzie and Harriet, Leave It to Beaver, Father Knows Best* and the *Donna Reed Show* promoted a white middle class cultural norm of male-headed households with wage earning being the responsibility of one man. The woman's role was that of ad hoc nurturer and unpaid household staff, cut off from aunts and uncles and generational support, dressed in perky shirtwaist dresses next to her avocado refrigerator and stove set. Honestly, very few people really fit this ideal, but that didn't stop them from trying!

Amos and Andy delivered an image of an African American urban culture at first portrayed on radio by white actors. These roles were racial and economic stereotypes of the harmless, borderline foolish, inner city good Negro. White working class roles were reinforced by The Honeymooners, in which Jackie Gleason's bus driver husband made light of domestic violence with so called comedic phrases like, "To the moon Alice, to the moon!" directed at his long-suffering wife. At the same time, a youth culture was literally constructed, and being a teenager became a consumer industry. Teenage shows like *American Bandstand* for the white kids and *Soul Train* for the black kids became wildly popular.

All of the roles in these media are intentionally constructed stereotypes – all of them! We were sold a bill of goods. We still are. What was going on inside people? Who knows! They were all stoned on the drugs of progress, alcohol, TV dinners, pharmaceuticals, patriotism, Youth Culture and The American Dream!

In the mid 1960's, the military draft jolted everyone out of consumer heaven and the incipient Age of Aquarius and into the hard cold reality that Uncle Sam wanted THEM to go to a country they had never heard of to kill or be killed. Some young men went into the military, others actively opposed the war, but no one escaped dealing with it.

Ten years later, Vietnam veterans returned home traumatized, disillusioned, and in many cases drug and alcohol addicted, anti war activists found themselves searching for meaning and a focus for life, and pretty soon thousands of Baby Boomers began flooding into 12-Step Programs to find community, spiritual support and to heal from the binge of the American Dream gone wrong.

AA became a new family of choice. The human need for extended family runs deep. Even cave paintings of prehistoric people show that we lived in clans long before written record.

We need a place to feel like we are part of something, to restore, to revive and heal, to laugh and cry, to protect one another from inner and outer enemies, a place where elders hold wisdom and tradition, young people are mentored, the elderly are respected and cared for and where generational wisdom is both valued and passed on. 12-Step programs restored a sense of community and order to the lives of thousands of lost children of the American Dream. A lot of people got better, many died from addictions or PTSD, but without a doubt, the beginning of a new social model was set in place.

But the hard sell had also become part of the air we breathed. We had become a nation of consumers. Advertising was, and still is, a multi-billion dollar industry, corporations increasingly replaced local industry, and Madison Avenue kept on selling the "get more, eat more, drink more, have more" culture to support the new market economy.

Addiction to work, booze, caffeine, speed, success, sex, fame, image, shopping, food, gambling, mood-changing substances of all kinds, prescription drugs, and to just plain MORE raged out of control. Consumerism replaced citizenship, shopping malls replaced churches and designer labels replaced real identity.

As people bottomed out and sought recovery, new consumers had to be hooked, and advertising targeted younger and younger demographic groups. But a new sub-culture had also begun, and the 12-Steps were part of it. Our country was searching for its soul, and spirituality, not religion, seemed to lead us back home and provide an antidote to a life of empty consumerism.

GOD AND THE 12-STEPS

Historically people have understood God differently as their worldview has changed. Following is a brief history of God:

- Animism – everything is alive, everything is God- led to
- Fertility Cults – the temple prostitute will guarantee a good crop- led to
- Tribal gods (we are the chosen people, and our god hates who we hate) – led to
- Gods of Olympus (a god for every occasion) – led to
- Monotheisms-Western, Middle Eastern, and Eastern, a Trinitarian God with a capital G-O-D.

While people's understandings of God may change as their world changes, direct experience of a living presence never changes. That's what folks mean when they say, "God is the same yesterday, today and tomorrow." They are describing the spiritual path.

This path of direct experience is also known as the way of the mystic. And in general, once you have had an experience of the Presence, you don't worry so much about what to call it. Organized religions have played an important part in nation building and creating stable societies worldwide. They help people define where they belong, and to create a safe zone where some of the stresses of the world can be healed. But in the United States, another major cultural shift is underway. Over 50% of Americans now say that they are "spiritual but not religious." At a time like this, many throw the baby out with the bathwater, and jump to another fast growing religion – atheism. But there is a middle way.

What are the elements of a gathered group, of two or three coming together for the purpose of spiritual transformation? And how do we define what we do together? Might the 12-Steps serve as a model? It makes good sense for us to look at what works about this simple 12-Step program of recovery, and to see how it might be made more accessible to people beyond the recovery community.

However we describe it, a spiritual paradigm shift is critical for recovery from a soul sickness, and addiction is such an illness. But a lot of recovering people are as far from wanting to jump into a religious conversation as Antarctica is from Planet Xenon. This path is different though, and the founders of AA describe it with amazing simplicity. *The Big Book of Alcoholics Anonymous* says it this way in the chapter *We Agnostics*:

> *Much to our relief, we discovered we did not need to consider another's conception of God. Our own conception, however inadequate, was sufficient to make the approach and to effect a contact with Him. As soon as we admitted the possible existence of a Creative Intelligence, a Spirit of the Universe underlying the totality of things, we began to be possessed of a new sense of power and direction, provided we took other simple steps. We found that God does not make too hard terms with those who seek Him. To us, the Realm of Spirit is broad, roomy, all-inclusive; never exclusive or forbidding to those who earnestly seek. It is open, we believe to all.*
>
> (Page 46, Alcoholics Anonymous)

The recovery program that became Alcoholics Anonymous, began one evening in a hotel lobby in Akron, Ohio, when one suffering alcoholic stretched out his hand to another. The Steps were not imposed, but discovered. It is described in "Dr. Bob and the Good Old Timers," that as people began to recover a little they saw that they needed to do inner healing and restitution in order to stay clean.

Since the first years of Alcoholics Anonymous, literally millions of people have been rescued from a lifetime of misery and addiction, through practicing the 12 "simple but not easy" Steps. Steps one through ten are inner and outer work on facing ourselves, and on restoration and healing. Step Eleven "Sought through prayer and meditation to improve our conscious contact with God as we understand God, praying only for knowledge of God's will for us, *and the power to carry it out*," opens a doorway inward, through which we find a conscious contact with the power of the Presence.

Inside that Step Eleven doorway, resides a lifetime of spiritual deepening. Once inside, we discover that we are finally "home." We still experience what every human does, including dark moments and times of doubt and pain, but once you penetrate "the secret place of the most high," you can always find your way home again. Inside this 11th Step doorway, we develop spiritual practices to reconnect us beyond the local or wounded self and back to Source, or Higher Power.

And then in Step-12, we pass it on.

SOME 12-STEP HISTORY

By the time the miracle of the 12-Steps appeared, people had been suffering with addictions for millennia with little relief. something happened one day in Akron, Ohio. Dr. Bob Smith and Bill Wilson, both alcoholics, one a physician and the other a mildly successful NY stockbroker, agreed to meet in a hotel lobby. The meeting was initiated by Bill Wilson, with the hope that something they might share with one another in that moment could keep each of them from drinking that day.

And yes, something did happen. That connection, of one hand reaching out to another in mutual support, has grown into a grass-roots, international psycho-spiritual miracle that has saved, and continues to save, the lives and sanity of millions.

Originally drawing from the six precepts of the Oxford Group and its heavy-duty fundamentalist Christianity, the early AA movement has evolved into a universal formula for body, mind, spirit healing. Something in the combination of energies of two very different, but equally committed men ignited a synergy that would not have been the same if only one of their approaches had prevailed. Ten Steps grew into 12-Steps, and something happened; a phenomenon was birthed! These Steps define a process for moving from despair and addiction into sobriety and altruistic purpose, and they really work.

Dr. Bob Smith pretty much stuck with the Oxford Group model his whole lifetime. Unfortunately he also suffered from life long depression and never lost the desire to drink either, so that would be what we call the white-knuckle approach. Actually, I would not be sober if that was the only way to go. I not only had a spiritual awakening, but also had the obsession to drink lifted from me, as have countless others. I think maybe Dr. Bob's path didn't include much joy, and joy is essential for a spiritual movement that works. Bless him for hanging in there in spite of his struggle.

Wilson on the other hand, a visionary and futurist, was excited about new and emerging ideas in the fields of metaphysics and science. He followed the work of Emmett Fox and the early Transcendentalists (Emerson, Thoreau), the "Mind-cure" movement described by William James in *Varieties of Religious Experience*, experimented with LSD, meditation and hypnosis and also understood that the illness of addiction was not just physical. He recognized that the new frontier beyond physical sobriety would need to be emotional sobriety, which set the stage for the family systems understanding of both addiction and recovery.

Wilson stayed "open at the top," as some metaphysical movements say, meaning open to continuing revelation and new ideas. But Dr. Bob grew the roots and held them in place, and together they channeled something greater than the sum of their individual abilities.

The balance between the two was genius. Think about it, a process developed by either of the founders alone could have produced either a depressed white knuckle Christianity or a wild-eyed experimental fiasco. But something both rooted and visionary was called forth through this particular combination of Smith and Wilson, a perfect example of synergy, which is when the sum of the parts equals more than one plus one.

Timing is everything. Clearly, a new idea was trying to emerge, and it wasn't just happening for alcoholics. Psychology had been largely focused on the abnormal, through the early work of Sigmund Freud, but leaders of the human potential movement like Carl Jung, Carl Rogers and Abraham Maslow began to develop a wellness model of human development. *Psycho-Cybernetics* by Maxwell Maltz, Abraham Maslow's *Hierarchy of Needs*, Erik Erikson's *Eight Ages of Man,* and others, augmented that work, and this new human potential movement slowly began to de-stigmatize the idea of psychotherapy and look at a developmental psychology for wholeness, not illness. This "possible human" cross-pollinated with the 12-Steps over time, and continues to change the way a whole nation looks at personal growth and spiritual life.

NEW THOUGHT AND THE 12-STEPS

Bill Wilson describes an inclusive spiritual path in the narrative of the book Alcoholics Anonymous. He derived the spiritual tone, language and basics of 12-Step spiritual philosophy from several sources. One is the bible. The paradoxical wisdom of the Beatitudes from Matthew 5, as taught in Emmet Fox's *Sermon on the Mount*, the New Testament books of James and 1st Corinthians constitute the biblical roots of 12-Step philosophy. Added to this is Hindu wisdom from the Bhagavad Gita, Jungian psychology and ideas from emerging physics. Together, these elements form the loosely formal foundation for what is known as "the spiritual part" of the AA program.

This may sound similar to New Thought spirituality. While there are many similarities, there are critical differences as well. Probably key among them is the fact that in 12-Step spirituality, personal recovery depends upon group unity, and this unity is based in a shared commitment to rebuilding broken people. New Thought tends to be uncomfortable with the broken part and the 12-Steps exist because of it. That is where hitting bottom comes in.

In 12-Step spirituality, your bottom is honestly your best friend. Conversely, New Thought isn't big on bottoms, and tends to focus on the light while de-emphasizing the dark, but anyone who has known the depths of despair needs a spirituality that can support the whole journey. Some of life's most valuable spiritual lessons are learned while navigating the dark night.

Denial of the shadow self, of so-called negative feelings and personality traits, is actually dangerous for recovering people. We can, and frankly must, face it all, and if our spiritual path is wide and deep enough, that is no problem. To use a Christian metaphor, Easter Sunday has to be preceded by Good Friday for the resurrection to take place. With this one exception in emphasis, however, New Thought spirituality is a natural complement to 12-Step Recovery.

WHAT IS NEW THOUGHT ANYWAY?

The roots of New Thought, a 20th Century religious movement, were decidedly Christian, but the interpretation, practical and metaphysical rather than literal. Starting in the late 1800's with the mind cure healings of Franz Mesmer – Mesmerism (hypnosis), the healing work of a clockmaker turned healer named Phineas Parkhurst Quimby, and Mary Baker Eddy – Christian Science, these teachings were recorded and put words to the practice, and a system began to emerge. Emma Curtis Hopkins, Charles and Myrtle Fillmore (Unity), Ernest Holmes (Religious Science) followed, and combined with the writings of the Transcendentalists (Emerson, Thoreau), to launch what became known as New Thought.

Here is a bit of interesting trivia. New Thought teachings were introduced into the Alcoholics Anonymous program because Bill Wilson's secretary was a student of Emmett Fox, and shared his weekly lectures in New York City and his writings on the Beatitudes, *The Sermon on the Mount*, with her boss. It's all about relationships!

New Thought is essentially metaphysical biblical interpretation, focusing on the God within (Jesus said the Kingdom of God is within), rather than a system of strict rules for social control attributed to a God in heaven. A basic principle of New Thought is that as a person transforms their consciousness, outer conditions automatically alter to reflect that reality. A biblical rendering of this idea is found in the Book of Proverbs, "as a man thinketh in his heart, so is he" (or she). One focuses then, upon the ideal or true nature of a thing or condition, rather than on the problem, and prays "from" a place of wholeness, and not "to" a power outside oneself. New Thought emphasizes human potential, use of spiritual mind treatments or affirmative prayer, the power of suggestion, affirmations and denials to enlist the cooperation of the subconscious mind in accessing Source.

New Thought is historically more interested in transcending and less in engaging social and justice issues or selfless service with those Jesus called "the least of these," but the people who transform through the miracle of the 12-Steps actually ARE the least of these when they start out! In my personal experience, a path of service not only makes a huge difference in individual lives, but also results in a win/win, a transcendence that also embodies. In plain English this means that not only do we change through surrender and reconnection, but when we also serve others by sharing our experience, strength and hope, we get to both have a spiritual awakening and give it away. Win-win.

Basic metaphysical principles like the Laws of Cause and Effect, The Law of Attraction and others, sometimes

> "What Mind can conceive,
> You can achieve"
>
> ERNEST HOLMES, SCIENCE OF MIND

become confused with magic bullet formulas that are largely about "manifesting" to the exclusion of practicing altruism, reciprocity and ego deflation. This can be misleading, as the fake versions incorporate quasi-spiritual language. A good way to recognize the difference between the two is this: If a teaching focuses on "getting," or "giving in order to get," it isn't the real deal. Those teachings aren't New Thought, and they are definitely the antithesis of 12-Step spirituality. They are more New Age than New Thought, but the line is very blurred between the two in popular culture.

One example is the popular film, "The Secret," that raged through the culture in 2006. Exposure to the idea of the Law of Attraction was a good thing, but a lot of people didn't have the background to interpret the deeper meaning of that metaphysical law and simplified it into a kind of cosmic get rich quick scheme; a glib promise of instant rewards for anyone who clicked their heels and wished hard.

There is, unfortunately, a danger in mistaking the real deal for a feel good bromide. In a fame obsessed, instant everything, five minutes of fame at any cost world, fake flowers can seem just as good as real ones. But if you want to bloom like a beautiful flower you can't skip the steps of planting a seed that holds the flower's potential, the breaking open of the seed to set the potential free, followed by the shooting of roots into the earth – and the crisis of the fulcrum, the peeping through the earth's surface of

the first green shoot. In nature, all of that pathos comes before the miracle of the fragrant bloom.

An artificial flower, while it does not fade away and die is not alive either. It will never bring the kind of ineffable beauty or fragrance into one day that a real flower will. This is where slogans that abound in the 12-Step programs really encourage us to stay the course.

"Half measures availed us nothing" is a favorite.

The coming-to-life process can be difficult. Honestly, it *is* difficult. Ask any mother. But the result is great! Life is what we are after, life more abundant, and that is what we gain access to if we hang in. Effortless victories are ultimately hollow anyway, and what you have at the end of the day is a fake flower without the majesty, pathos, peril or drama of "the journey of becoming" living in its petals. You want to be a juicy beautiful Daffodil or Hyacinth, or Bird of Paradise, right?

The idea of all wisdom teachings is for us to get in alignment with our Source, with the flow of good, of substance, of life, and to trust that once in that flow, we are both agents and recipients of Divine Love. We get into alignment with our Source and we begin to resonate with a vibration that magnetizes more of that to us. This is the essence of the Law of Attraction.

So to recap, we need to be willing to go

deep, fall apart if necessary, break open and allow for uncertainty and pain if indicated, in order to be reborn. The process can feel scary, but nets great and lasting rewards, and some of the best stuff lies deep within the void. So we need to be willing to embrace both the light and the dark, and in so doing, will find our way back to who we really are. Fake shortcuts just don't work, and there are numerous programs and hard sells out there that mimic the path but promise a less pain, more gain result.

Hitting bottom is our greatest gift, and sometimes we hit a few bottoms before we decide to surrender. When we finally do, we discover a trampoline at the bottom that bounces us into a new place. We never have to do any of this alone. There are always fellow travelers along the 12-Step recovery route who have been where we are afraid to go, and will walk every step with us if we ask. Asking them to help us, helps them, and this is only one of the paradoxical miracles of this path. Do not fear the dark, for it is where the light is born.

In musical language, we need the bass note as well as the treble to make a chord that supports a symphony of recovery.

The teachings of the wisdom path are usually hidden in plain sight, and are most frequently told through metaphor and story. Sacred books like the Bible, the Bhagavad Gita, the Upanishads, the Yoga Sutras, the Koran, and others contain stories that draw us more deeply into the realm of power. These mythic texts have lasted over time because they are channeled containers for Truth. Reading, studying, reflecting upon and really using the ancient texts is a way to deeply connect to our own inner wisdom path.

There are many wisdom texts, but they are all paths that lead to a direct contact with Source. The texts themselves are not divine but they are tools to reach the divine. To be clearer than clear, the Bible and the Koran are both tools, the 12-Steps, Yoga, Chanting, Music for trance etc. are tools, the Big Book of AA, the Daily Word are tools. They are all tools for you to utilize to go deeper into YOU and discover the Truth, the Eternal Presence and Power, the Source of all creation...the living Spirit, the God within.

"Worship the Light, not the Lamp."
-Bahá'u'lláh

This Baha'i saying basically means don't confuse the teacher with the wisdom they teach. Don't get hung up on super star teachers or deify any book, but rather take from their teachings what you can use, internalize the message, and trust God to do the work of transformation.

12-STEPS AS WISDOM TEXT

Truth teachings are found in every culture. No one path has a monopoly on God. Jesus tells teaching stories called parables about everyday human encounters and nature, and they can be understood on many levels. We understand more as we become more tuned in to their vibration, and no amount of forcing the issue will work. Jesus explains to his disciples that he is modeling and transmitting the deeper levels of his teachings to them in private, but they still don't get it until he dies. If you actually read the bible, you will discover that Jesus had quite a temper at times, and was frustrated beyond belief at the seeming obtuseness in the disciples. It seems to be a universal truth that when we develop eyes to see and ears to hear the deeper wisdom, it reveals itself to us, and not a second sooner. Sometimes you can read a story many times and then one day you just get it, you understand something on a deeper level that had eluded you until that second. This is where regular spiritual practice of some sort

comes in. Intentional practice opens a channel through which deeper wisdom can be accessed.

Like biblical parables, Zen kōans are also teaching stories, meant to broaden insight into Buddhist teachings. Presented in the form of a question like, "What is the sound of one hand clapping?," the surface level of the teaching may seem nonsensical, but there are deeper truths to be discovered through the contemplation of the query. The difference between wisdom texts and just any old book, is that the wisdom text possesses this multivalent quality of many layers of meaning.

The same thing is true with the 12-Steps. On the surface they are a recovery program for treating addictions, but hidden within their deeper practice and subtler teaching are layers of Truth. My spiritual search has led me to study and practice many paths, but I keep coming back to the 12-Steps as the default. You could say that rather than going wider, I have gone deeper.

I have studied the Bible, the Gnostic Gospels and other wisdom texts in depth, as well as indigenous spiritual traditions and the 12-Steps, and have come to feel that the 12-Steps closely resonate with the Jesus Path, as hinted at in the bible, and made more explicit in the Nag Hammadi Scrolls. The scrolls open a window onto the teachings of the Jewish Jesus, an Afro-Asiatic, Near Eastern wisdom teacher, a social and political radical who is a service oriented healer. The teachings of the Buddha and those of Krishna in the Hindu B'hagavad Gita are also extremely close to both the teachings of Jesus of the Nag Hammadi Scrolls and the principles of the 12-Step program.

The Bible most of us know is the result of extensive political re-writing and elimination of numerous early texts that hint at the spiritual practice of the Jesus Movements that proliferated after Jesus died. The resulting approved biblical canon, along with a "systematic theology" that describes a storyline that is utterly fabricated, in which Jesus somehow has a death wish and dies "for our sins" has become the backbone of Western Christianity. In fact, he was a reformer and critic of the Roman Empire, and a defender of the poor and the outcast.

But even through this crazy misappropriation of the teaching and spirit of Jesus, the power of the core wisdom teachings in both the Old and New Testaments has stayed alive. The movement for "life more abundant" through serving "the least of these" continues to live and transform lives in spite of years of theological efforts to obscure the essential nature of the path.

Theologian Howard Thurman is the voice I first heard that differentiated the Jesus Path from the doctrine of Christianity. Thurman, an influential African American author, philosopher, theologian, civil rights leader and powerful preacher, who started the Church for the Fellowship of All Peoples in San Francisco in the 1940's, along with a white co-Pastor, and was later the Dean of Chapel at both Howard University and Boston University, said he was not a Christian, but a follower of the teachings of Jesus. That made a lot of sense to me.

Thurman was interested in a lived spiritual path based on the Jesus Path, and made a huge effort to realize that dream as the Beloved Community in his diverse ministry experiment of more than fifteen years. It was heartbreaking for Dr. Thurman when some of his members were among the Japanese American citizens rounded up and put into concentration camps during World War ll. The church community was not able to either save them from the fate of incarceration or create a meaningful witness to oppose the action. Culture and politics interfered with the creation of Thurman's Beloved Community. But the spiritual power of the Jesus Path has prevailed through millennia in spite of both political and theological attempts to snuff it out.

This Jesus Path can definitely be intuited by reading the Bible, but so many political agendas and literary styles collide in the final canon of that book, and formal doctrines confuse the question further. Most people just aren't interested in trying to separate the path from the propaganda, and who could blame them! It wasn't until I was a graduate student of Religion at Claremont School of Theology that I began to find my way into the inner sanctum and the heart of the earliest biblical texts, and to find a way into what seems to be that Jesus Path.

ANCIENT SCROLLS SHED LIGHT

The Nag Hammadi Scrolls, sometimes called the Gnostic Gospels, were discovered, or actually re-discovered in Egypt in 1945. They include the books of Thomas, Mary Magdalene and Judas among others, and seem to fill in a lot of the spirit and human relational side of the early Jesus movements. The Book of Thomas in particular opens a door to a richer complexity in some familiar biblical stories.

When I was a little girl, my grandmother's minister, Mr. Vail, "gave" me a scripture, I was about five years old and after meeting me he looked into my eyes and said, "'Ask and it shall be given unto you, seek and you shall find, knock and it shall be opened unto you', Matthew 7:7. That is your scripture." OK. I never forgot it, but frankly the whole thing seemed a bit remote to me. Even at five years old, I had endured suffering. I knew that if it were just a matter of "asking," my parents would not be divorced, my mother would not be so sad, unpredictable and preoccupied, and I would be spending most of my days with my grandparents where I felt safe and seen. I asked that these things be fixed every day. And they weren't.

Years later, after many lessons and many more sufferings, I finally discovered the same teaching Matthew 7:7 describes, in the Nag Hammadi scroll Book of Thomas, and it filled in a lot of blanks. From the Book of Thomas, v1-2:

Prologue: These are the secret sayings that the living Jesus spoke and Didymus John Thomas recorded.

1. *And he said, "Whoever discovers the interpretation of these sayings will not taste death."*
2. *Jesus said, "Those who seek should not stop seeking until they find. When they find, they will be disturbed. When they are disturbed they will be amazed, and will rule over all."*

Wait a minute! Now, THIS makes sense! This still promises that you will find something of value if you ask. But it doesn't give you artificial flowers. This teaching includes the whole drama of planting the seed, watering the seed, nurturing the plant and staying faithful to the daily growth of that plant (or consciousness). Thomas's text describes a *process* of becoming. There is effort and darkness and sometimes breaking and even despair involved in this asking and seeking. And the promise is that IF we can hang in there and learn what the pain of "being disturbed" has to offer, we will not only be amazed, but we will "rule over all."

"Ruling over all" means we develop the power to activate dominion over our own mind.

This ruling over all is the opening of the third eye of wisdom about which the mystics teach. When we are "seeing rightly," the turbulence of depression, or the setbacks of life, will not ultimately defeat us.

The biblical teaching in Matthew 7:7 is just too slick. Like the movie *The Secret*, it tells us that if we seek we shall find – instant success with limited effort. But it leaves out the "being troubled" part, and that is a big part of the journey. There are valuable lessons to be learned from the darkness as well as from the Light. Ultimately, we recognize that it is all Light, but we do that by understanding the contrast in the darkness and the light. This Jesus Path mirrors the 12-Step process of inner work.

But how do we manage the journey inward without breaking? And where can we find the courage to undergo yet another step inward when we discover painful places along the way? The 12-Step program has an answer for that. The key is in the word "we." In 12-Step recovery and spirituality we are never asked to do it alone, and with the proper support and guidance, we actually grow stronger in the broken places. Remember, in a 12-Step community of recovering people, personal recovery depends upon working with others and giving service in community. With the help and support of fellow journeyers on the path, we develop the courage to look within. The deeper we go on this journey, the closer we get to freedom.

By the way, there is actually something to be said for struggling. Human babies develop crucial immune responses by struggling through the birth canal. The process of spiritual birth can sometimes seem as treacherous as that first time around. Spiritual awakening through the Steps is a kind of second birth and it nets amazing rewards if we trust the process. This is I believe what Jesus is referring to when he says that in order to enter the Kingdom of God, we must be born again. This is an inner spiritual birth into that Kingdom, to the God within, and it is very worth the struggle.

The 12-Steps provide one roadmap for this rebirth, community provides the support for the under-taking, and the power of healing is activated and sustained by beginning.

Every journey really does begin with the first step.

JESUS AND THE 12-STEPS

In 1946, just one year after the discovery of the Nag Hammadi Scrolls, the first scrolls from another library of original first century texts was discovered at Qumran, near the Dead Sea, in Palestine. These scrolls are a collection of first testament Jewish documents, the library of a second temple sect known as the Essenes. Both the Nag Hammadi and the Dead Sea Scrolls open new windows into understanding the lived essence and culture of early first century Judaism.

The Dead Sea Scroll community at Qumran was a group of religious purists who were very different from either the temple Jews or the Gnostic community near Nag Hammadi. There is no question that the world of the Gnostics is much more appealing to a mystic than the stringent dualist teachings of the monastic first century cult at Qumran, but it is fascinating to learn from these texts how Jewish religion was behaving in the years after the death of Jesus, and as Christianity was forming.

The fact that all three of these systems — the 12-Steps in 1935, the scrolls in 1945 and 1946, were "discovered" at roughly the same moment in history doesn't seem coincidental to me. It seems mystical, and like a major gift to humankind. So bottom line, the bible your grandmother knew is not the bible we understand today. More has been revealed.

And much like the difference between the Dr. Bob path and the Bill Wilson road in Alcoholics Anonymous, there were multiple ways to go in the Jewish first century, and the Gnostic Gospels, or Nag Hammadi Scrolls, reveal a lived path that is strikingly similar to the lived spirituality of the 12-Steps.

To be clear, Jesus was not a Christian, and neither do you have to be, to engage the transformational healing and wisdom of this Afro Asiatic Ancient Near Eastern embodiment of the Christ. Jesus was a Jew who never heard of Christianity and didn't try to start any religion,

> "If you bring forth what is within you, what you have will save you. If you do not have that within you, what you do not have within you will kill you."
>
> BOOK OF THOMAS, VERSE 70

but he did have an urgent message of unconditional love to get across. This Jewish Jesus was also culturally a child of questionable parentage, living in a deeply traditional Jewish society, and his path of lived compassion incorporates a first hand understanding of what it is like to be an outsider. He has an uncanny grasp of power relationships, and a great distaste for misuse of authority. He teaches from nature and human stories, hangs out with marginalized people and emphasizes equity for widows and untouchables. He accesses and teaches the transforming power of unconditional love, and even in the worst moments of a tough life, he triumphs over pettiness and hatred.

He dies and then lives. He endures a brutal murder, and in three days is walking around in his etheric body, with his disciples. And before he moves on into the spirit realm, he walks them through the process of his transfiguration so that they can become empowered too. He is the real deal.

Jesus lived in a time when Roman rule was utterly oppressive in Ancient Israel, and he was an observant Jew who understood the teachings of Torah in a way that threatened the temple status quo. The head rabbi of the temple worked with the Roman leaders to keep the Jewish people docile, paying their tribute to the Roman government. The temple rabbis lead a life of luxury as part of the deal, and Jesus was a teacher who challenged this paradigm.

Jesus was part of a tradition of roaming wisdom teachers in his time in history. He teaches through story, through parable, and through actions. The stories he tells can be utilized on many levels, as can all wisdom teachings. He gathers a group of disciples, as was common for the nomadic wisdom teacher in his time, but much of the deeper meaning of his teachings is lost on them. He tells the disciples the deeper truths in his private times with them, and even so, they largely miss the point.

Much of the dynamic power of The Jesus Path can be learned through reading his interactions with his disciples and with those he encounters along the way.

However he did it, Jesus opened a powerful energetic pathway to the Divine Source. It is amazing to realize that even though the deeper keys to his teachings were extracted from the "official" documents about Christianity and then hidden, they have resurfaced in an era when humankind is ready to re-integrate them.

One of the most powerful stories about Jesus and his method for focusing us inward as a way to access power is found in the story of the man at the Bethesda Fountain, found in John 5: 1-16.

The Bethesda Fountain was known for its healing properties. The central character in the biblical story about this fountain is a man who almost gets himself to the place where his breakthrough can happen, and then gets stuck. The legend says that the "healing angel" troubles the water at a certain time every day, and if you can get into the waters at that moment, you will be healed. This man has been waiting there for thirty-eight years for someone to help him into the pool. Thirty-eight years!

Thirty-eight years is plenty of time to form an identity. And his identity is one of victim on top of victim. He has basically set up residence adjacent to the place of his breakthrough, and then has refined his story about why he CAN'T break through. Have you ever done that? A lot of folks get stuck just before the breakthrough. This man sure did!

In thirty-eight years you can really get comfortable in an uncomfortable way. You can set up some patterns that are hard to want to leave. Everybody knew where to find him. He was always at the Bethesda Fountain. He probably knows all of the news of the day, and gets a lot of interesting stories from the people who come to the fountain to be healed. He probably has his Starbucks delivered daily and knows just how to get the sympathy going so that people give him pity, and even paid him for his disability.

So when Jesus comes upon this man, he asks him a life-changing question:

"Do you *want* to be made whole?"

In the pregnant silence that follows, there exists drama and pathos and unlimited potential. Actually, in this moment is the living heart and soul of the Jesus message. It is also the key to your moment of breakthrough, and the essential question of 12-Step recovery:

"Do *you* want to be made whole?"

It is not an easy question to answer. The man at the fountain might ask: "If I say yes, what do I have to give up? And what will replace it?"

Another question might be "Who will I be if I am not the guy at the fountain for thirty-eight years? Do I have an identity beyond that of my disability?"

But if he says no, he will never be able to be the same oblivious victim again. He will know that he had a choice, he had a moment, and that he chose not to risk leaving his uncomfortable comfort zone for the uncertainty of a breakthrough.

Nature cannot tolerate a vacuum. Neither can most people it seems. We fill up on food and sex and drugs and crazy schedules and Facebook, the second we clear out a little space for something new to happen inside of us. We do a lot to keep from feeling the emptiness.

But if we want to be made whole, we have

> "Are you ready to be made whole?"
>
> JOHN 5:6

to be willing to empty ourselves regularly of outworn identities and ideas, of old hurts and resentments, of prejudices and self-defeating behaviors. And if we really want to be made whole, we have to be able to tolerate the emptiness between the emptying and the filling up.

Jesus says that the answer is within. So to be made whole, inward is where we need to look. Actually, we all want to be made whole. We all want to be made whole because we start out whole, and there is something in each of us that is always homesick for our true nature until we finally get back to it.

But when we find ourselves a million miles from that home within, and don't have a clue how to get back there, finding our way back can seem pretty impossible. Do not give up. Give in. To be made whole in the case of that man at the fountain, or you or me, means being willing to let go of old storylines and comfort zones.

It requires courage, and making a choice. It requires commitment, and a willingness to invest the time in your own transformation. It requires being ready for something new, and letting go of old associations and activities that hold you at a lower vibratory level.

Transformation is a process, not a destination. Asking the man if he wanted to be made whole opened the door for a process to begin. I would suggest that the man knew that already, which is why he had waited for over thirty years. He wasn't sure he was up for the challenge, but for some reason this day he was ready to say yes. And that changed everything.

Are you ready? What might get you ready?

Don't worry about results, just focus on the journey. We live in a results obsessed age, and too many "get rich quick," overnight fame schemes have infiltrated our mass consciousness. But honestly this isn't the way it works. An insight can change everything in an instant, but internalizing lasting change is a process. And the journey IS the destination!

Constantine's version of Christianity actually did an amazing sleight-of-hand trick. The Jesus we know through orthodox Christianity is a Romanized version of a thoroughly non-Roman rabbi. For starters, the ethnicity is wrong! A blond haired, blue-eyed weak looking guy surrounded by little white children is the image we see in White and Black and Asian churches all over America. The historical Jesus was a man of color, who took on the established order, served social outcasts like widows and women and lepers, exposed the corruption of temple priests who were in collusion with the Roman authorities in oppressing the Jewish people, and was actually killed because of it. It is likely that he was a magnet for children as the picture depicts, but not as a weak passive white guy with blond hair. The depth path of Jesus was that of a spiritual warrior,

"Be ye transformed by the renewal of your mind."

ROMANS 12:2

a political revolutionary and a teacher of radical love of both neighbor and self.

There were almost 400 years between when Jesus died and Constantine totally appropriated the diverse spiritual communities known as the "Jesus Movements," along with Jesus's name, for his "Roman Empire brand." Constantine was a brilliant guy really. He basically franchised Jesus – a "things go better with Coke" kind of thing. Of course, the thing about franchises is that they have great marketing teams, and so this "official church" is the one that made it into the mind of popular western culture. The Jesus who is an enlightened master, wisdom teacher, social activist and radical advocate for the poor and marginalized is not easy to find amidst the bishops and power struggles, sexism, homophobia, original sin and threats of hell in too many organized churches.

Christian mystics over the ages, from Meister Eckhart to Martin Luther King Jr., and Thomas Merton have understood, taught and lived the wisdom teachings of Jesus, but they were marginalized and excommunicated and sometimes even killed for doing so. The Muslim tradition honors Jesus as a great teacher, and some esoteric Indian sects even claim that he was initiated in yogic depth teachings during the years between age 12 and 30 when he disappears from the biblical narrative. The version of Jesus in these traditions is perhaps closer to the heart of the historic Jesus, as they are not under the pressure to promote the brand.

Other traditions suggest that Jesus went not to India, but rather to Egypt for those years between 12 and 30. Wherever he went during the interim, the Jesus who emerges at age 30 to model for us an embodied, lived altruistic path of enlightenment for only three years and to share the deep vibratory healing of the prayer he taught in the tonal language he spoke, Aramaic, was and is an awesome realized master.

The Jesus Path that emerges through the Nag Hammadi scrolls is an inner way, or path of self-knowledge and radical love. It calls us to summon the courage to weather the journey through the valley of the shadow of death and leaves us with an imperative to share the resultant spiritual awakening, by sharing the message and being of service among "the least of these."

Sounds like the 12-Steps to me!

"Beyond our ideas of right-doing and wrong-doing,
there is a field. I'll meet you there.
When the soul lies down in that grass,
the world is too full to talk about.
Ideas, language, even the phrase 'each other'
doesn't make sense any more."

RUMI

COMMUNITY AND THE 12-STEPS

Traditional churches and synagogues are increasingly out of step with the culture and are emptying out at a great rate, but we still need community. We are hard wired, as humans, to connect, and we experience synergy power when we connect in community. Jesus said that where two or more are gathered in the name of God, there will that power be also. So the question becomes how to find or found a community, where health and personal growth are encouraged, where wisdom of the elders nurtures the generations, and neurosis is minimal. Your community of choice might be called a church, synagogue or sangha. It might be called a theatre company, a spiritual center, a classroom or Meet Up group or an 11th Step Workshop or salon. What it's called isn't as important as what it makes possible.

Dr. Martin Luther King Jr. popularized the concept of the Beloved Community, in which diversity at every level is embraced. The key quality that needs to be present in your Beloved Community, your Tribe, your support community of choice, is altruism – for the members to have mutual commitment to the growth, development and unfolding of the greatest good for all of its members and for the world. This is a community of synergy, where one and one can equal ten.

The 12-Steps are the Beloved Community in action. Teachers, sponsors and mentors show up when we are ready. You will find a teacher. You will probably find a few teachers. One day you will resonate with someone or with a particular teaching and you will open to your inner wisdom...and when you find that person or teaching, you will know. That will be your Guru, your Rabbi. And a true guru will point you back to your real teacher...your own inner voice of deep intuition, which connects you to Divine Mind, Source, God.

At this point it is probably good to look

> "Having had a spiritual awakening as the result of these steps we tried to carry this message to others and practiced these principles in all of our affairs."
>
> STEP-12, ALCOHOLICS ANONYMOUS

at the difference between healing and cure. The debate is inconclusive at a scientific level about whether addicts and alcoholics can really be "cured." Some people choose to call themselves *recovered* and not **recovering**. The disease model suggests that once an alcoholic or other kind of addict, always an alcoholic or addict. There are anecdotal horror stories about people who return to drinking after thirty years of sobriety and become hopeless drunks or die in two weeks. Because I know that I have a physical sensitivity to alcohol and drugs, and a mind that sometimes tells me I am just fine even when I am not. I don't really care to tempt fate and see if I am cured. But I *have* been healed. So can you be.

Bill Wilson wrote about "the next frontier," of growth beyond the 12-Steps, as that of "emotional sobriety," but he did not live to see the emergence of his legacy of the family systems and wellness movement of the 12-Step Nation.

After getting sober and stable through the steps, and once you have landed on solid ground, you may find yourself craving a way into the depth teaching and God realization of the 11th Step and beyond. There are many traditions and tools that can aid your practice.

Whatever the individual elements of healing are that came together to create the 12-Step model, it is clear that there is more here than meets the eye. The 12-Steps are a model for a universal spiritual path, a lifelong holistic psycho/spiritual/ethical lived Path reflective of the Jesus Path, the Buddha Path, wisdom teachings of Kabbalah and Krishna, the Christian mystics, depth psychology of Carl Jung and the human potential work of Abraham Maslow and others.

And the rewards of embarking on the Path are great. After the work of the first nine steps is complete, the writers of the 12-Steps present us with a list of fabulous Promises. They are offered as a developmental certainty, if one has worked the preceding Steps, and are nothing short of miraculous for people who have been mired in despair and addiction. Actually they are pretty miraculous for anyone!

THE PROMISES:

If we are painstaking about this phase of our development, we will be amazed before we are half way through.

We are going to know a new freedom and a new happiness.

We will not regret the past nor wish to shut the door on it.

We will comprehend the word serenity and we will know peace. No matter how far down the scale we have gone, we will see how our experience can benefit others.

That feeling of uselessness and self-pity will disappear. We will lose interest in selfish things and gain interest in our fellows.

Self-seeking will slip away. Our whole attitude and outlook upon life will change.

Fear of people and of economic insecurity will leave us.

We will intuitively know how to handle situations which used to baffle us.

We will suddenly realize that God is doing for us what we could not do for ourselves.

Are these extravagant promises? We think not. They are being fulfilled among us – sometimes quickly, sometimes slowly. They will always materialize if we work for them.

(pages 83, 84 Alcoholics Anonymous)

UNDERSTANDING THE 12-STEPS AS SPIRITUAL PRACTICE

Re-connecting to Source, restoring through surrender, digging deep, releasing, making amends and giving back in community is a simple way to describe the basic 12-Step spiritual path. The Steps provide structure for our inward seeking so we can relax and surrender and let the journey unfold. On a path, we don't need to reinvent the wheel every single day. This 12-Step path is practical too, "a design for living when the going gets rough," as the AA *Big Book* says.

The journey is individual, but the path is not solitary. Community makes all the difference. And when we finally get home, we begin to grow up. And through it all, practicing the 12-Steps over and over, deeper and deeper, an inner ecology and balance emerge as the new set point where pain and sadness used to live.

Developmental psychologists of the human potential movement, Carl Rogers and Abraham Maslow and psychologist Carl Jung all teach that in order to build a strong inner person, we may have to go back to fill in some blanks in our early development. Jung also teaches that humans have an intrinsic need to experience ecstatic states, but that before soaring we had better secure a strong foundation.

It has been said that everybody builds castles in the air, but some of us move in. Drugs and alcohol are a shortcut to the castle in the air, but the high doesn't last, the come down isn't pretty, and the roots aren't stable. Practicing the 12-Steps as spiritual practice creates a scaffolding to support us while we fill in developmental blanks. And the Steps are a great way to get to the castle in the air too.

Early recovery is a balancing act. Getting a foundation going, figuring out a connection to a non-drug source of ecstasy, and then basically changing everything in our whole lives, while trying to function in our jobs, in the world, and with our loved ones is no easy game, and added

> ## "The Universe will reward you for taking risks on its behalf."
>
> -SHAKTI GAWAIN

upon, will build your spiritual scaffolding. Combine these steps with Sacred Service, and elements like color, light, sound, vibration and gemstones, and you will create a support system for a lifetime of spiritual growth.

to that is the fact that we are healing on more than one level. This is where the spiritual element of recovery comes into play and in truth, saves the day.

If you think about spiritual energy traveling in a spiral upward, it is easy to visualize how a system like the 12-Steps heals holistically. Each Step involves self-examination through a particular lens, shedding what's not working, assimilating what is, and springing forward or upward to the next level. Think of trees shedding leaves to complete the cycle of life held in their DNA. To be fully alive, we need to let go of old ideas as much as trees do of leaves in the fall.

The 12-Steps heal multi-dimensionally. Shamans of many cultures reconnect and integrate strands of ancestral DNA in both the individual and their ancestral tribe through ritual and prayerful practices. Their work heals and knits together on the physical, etheric and ancestral planes, and so does the work of the 12-Steps.

Again, there are many paths, but one destination. Now let's look at the basics of a 12-Step Spirituality. First we will talk about Principles, and then Practices, and you will begin to see how using these basics as your structure, along with some of the systems we have already touched

SOME 12-STEP UNIVERSAL SPIRITUAL PRINCIPLES:

- God is good and omnipresent.
- How we see God is how we see our world.
- If we believe that Source/God is good, our world will reflect that.
- Words have power.
- Our self-talk shapes and reflects our inner environment, emanates naturally from our core beliefs. As we change our thinking we change our lives.
- How we treat one another matters.
- Our destinies are intertwined.
- You can't keep it unless you give it away.
- Gratitude and humility are powerful forces for healing and for good.
- Service to others transforms and heals.

THE 12-STEPS

1. We admitted we were powerless over alcohol – that our lives had become unmanageable.
2. Came to believe that a Power greater than ourselves could restore us to sanity.

3. Made a decision to turn our will and our lives over to the care of God, as we understood Him.

4. Made a searching and fearless moral inventory of ourselves.

5. Admitted to God, to ourselves, and to another human being the exact nature of our wrongs.

6. Were entirely ready to have God remove all these defects of character.

7. Humbly asked Him to remove our shortcomings.

8. Made a list of all persons we had harmed, and became willing to make amends to them all.

9. Made direct amends to such people wherever possible, except when to do so would injure them or others.

10. Continued to take personal inventory, and when we were wrong, promptly admitted it.

11. Sought through prayer and meditation to improve our conscious contact with God as we understood Him, praying only for knowledge of His will for us and the power to carry that out.

12. Having had a spiritual awakening as the result of these steps, we tried to carry this message to alcoholics, and to practice these principles in all our affairs.

The 12-Steps work in order. Practiced with some regularity, these inner ecological tools literally transform us at the cellular level. If you decide to take this journey inward, expect to run into parts of yourself you might not want to look at. There is an eastern wisdom tradition that talks about "threshold guards." Some people call it the devil, others the "not God force." Whatever you call them, these guards try to throw us off the path in a thousand ways. They may come in the form of people telling you they hate your ideas, or who do you think you are to have big dreams and aspirations? They may even say they hate *you*. At times they will seem to be growling at you. Expect the threshold guards, in whatever form they appear. Befriend them. They don't have any power in the face of Light.

Here is another paradox! The deeper you go, the higher you can reach. And the answer really is in your next footstep. Remember, your efforts are supported by a silent partner, with unlimited power. Keep going. Go deeper and elevate, elevate, elevate.

Actually making it to the threshold guards is a good sign! Joseph Campbell in *The Hero with a Thousand Faces* tells us that the archetypal Hero's, or Heroine's Journey has predictable rhythm and stages. The road often gets darker just before a breakthrough. Keep going! In the darkest moment, you possess all of the ingredients you need to make the very next step your springboard for transformation. The point of power is in the present moment.

Here is a hint. The truth that will "save" you is inside of you.

THE GATEWAYS

Think of the 12-Steps as a
scaffolding or ladder to support
your spiritual spine.

HOW TO USE
THE GATEWAYS

The Gateways are a system of energies and practices that support each step on the inner ladder.

Each Gateway combines the deeper essence of one of the 12-Steps, and includes a holistic tool kit of spiritual practices, including a Chakra, a Chinese Meridian, color, sound, gemstone, musical note and a ritual to support each level inward and onward. Each level also correlates with a part of the body, a psycho-spiritual layer of energy, and the organs and energies that correspond to that vibratory level.

The process of deeper spiritual journeying is like the peeling off of the thin membrane of one layer of an onion at a time. Once you are on the journey, you will naturally be drawn onto the next step. Sometimes what you discover there is discomfort. That is natural! You are penetrating the secret place of the most high, the inner sanctuary, the place where your essential self has always lived. The practice of this inner path is meant to be both creative and enjoyable, and

to open you to new possibilities. The Gateways are designed to provide you with many different tools that resonate with each stage of your journey.

To go along with the Gateways, I have created a Holistic Bento Box of Body/Mind/Spirit tools to introduce you to some additional supportive practices for spiritual capacity building. The word holistic comes from the root word whole. We simply cannot heal from our separation from Source without addressing all parts of ourselves. A bento refers to a single portion meal common in Japanese Cuisine. A typical Japanese bento box may hold rice, fish or meat, pickled or cooked vegetables.

This Holistic Inter-Spiritual Bento Box menu contains Mind, Body and Spirit tools for transformation. Pick one or more from each group and enjoy the feast! The Body, Mind, Spirit tools in the Bento Box can be useful in your private devotional times, or can be used in a more formal service or gathering. To paraphrase the *Big Book*, this list is meant to be suggestive only. As you travel the road to happy destiny, you will find tools and practices that work for you.

The Gateways flow naturally in sequence, and each one includes a deeper exploration of each of the 12-Steps. They can be used when we encounter a physical or emotional challenge, or are formally working a Step. For instance, along my journey I have repeatedly encountered illness or injury in my Second Chakra area. This is the area that correlates with Maslow's Generativity stage, and physically contains the reproductive organs, the hips, which are the way we move forward, or not, and is also the site of the lower back, of profound desires to birth a dream and to express deepest longings. I have actually had surgeries, done energy work, used crystals, chanting, music, and movement all relating to this Second Chakra level, "Came to believe that a Power Greater than ourselves could restore us to sanity." So this is a personal level I work over and over. I have stayed in the game, but it has been a real struggle at times! And the Gateways are a way of sharing with you how I have used the multi-dimensional tools that particularly resonate at each stage. So when you encounter your area of resistance, it is my hope that you will not turn back, but will rather find tools in one of the Gateways to support that stage of unpeeling.

Some questions as you prepare to embark on the inner walk:

Are you ready for something truly new?

Are you prepared to weather the journey inward?

Are you ready to be made whole?

So just to recap:

Step One is about acknowledging anything over which we are powerless, and admitting it isn't working for us. It may be a kind of communication pattern, a habitual choice of relationship, or an addictive process of any kind. Whatever it is that isn't working, after admitting that in Step One, we begin a process. We surrender to a Higher Power, clean house, make amends, seek conscious contact with Source, through the 11th Step, through prayer and meditation, opening the door to a lifetime daily practice of the Presence. And in Step 12 we take the awakening back into the world, sharing our gift through service to others, and we pass on the story of our experience, strength and hope to anyone who might benefit. That's the Gateways in a nutshell!

RITUAL AS A HEALING TOOL

Ritual is a Sacred Art in which Intention Is Everything. It has been said that without ritual there is no community. A sacred ritual is simply an action undertaken with the intention to connect to a deeper part of ourselves and to our Source and involves consecrating or setting aside time and intention for a holy purpose. Even everyday acts undertaken with great care and intention can be a sacred ritual.

Saying a common prayer at the end of a meeting or service is a ritual. Early AA meetings all ended with the recitation of The Lord's Prayer, and the practice continues to this day. I have joked with friends over the years that maybe what really works after all is just standing around holding hands and saying that prayer!

The Neil Douglas Klotz poetic translation of the Jesus Prayer, or Lord's Prayer, from the Aramaic, brings back the vibratory power of the original. This prayer is widely known as "the prayer that Jesus taught." When Jesus says, "When you pray, pray like this…" he means more than words. He is transmitting a vibratory healing system. Aramaic is a tonal language, and this prayer said in the original tongue will ring your being.

Even said aloud in an English translation of the Greek, the prayer retains a power, but the original language and mystical layered meanings really up the ante!

The Lord's Prayer from the Aramaic,
Translation; Neil Douglas-Klotz

*"O cosmic Birther of all
radiance and vibration.*

*Soften the ground of our being
and carve out a space within us
where your presence can abide.*

*Fill us with your creativity so that
we may be empowered to bear
the fruit of your mission.*

*Let each of our actions bear fruit
in accordance with your desire.*

*Endow us with the wisdom to
produce and share what each being
needs to grow and flourish.*

*Untie the tangled threads of destiny
that bind us, as we release others from
the entanglement of past mistakes.*

*Do not let us be seduced by that
which would divert us from our
true purpose, but illuminate the
opportunities of the present moment.*

*For you are the ground and
fruitful vision, the birth, power
and fulfillment, as all is gathered
and made whole once again."*

This translation from the Aramaic, rather than from the Greek to English, retains the power, poetry and depth, transcends the Christian interpretation and draws directly on the esoteric power of the original prayer. Intoning it, even in the less poetic form, both activates and grounds the process of deep inner work and transformation that are the essence of the 12-Step practice in communal meetings, prayer, meditation and a life of service.

Other rituals can be as simple as walking in nature in high awareness, creating order through washing dishes mindfully, or the Feng Shui art of placement, lighting candles on an altar, or striking a singing bowl. "What I know, what my body knows, even if my mind cannot remember it," is a good way to understand Ritual. Practicing some sacred ritual imprints a deeper connection to the One at the cellular level. Each Gateway will suggest one possible ritual for you to use, and you will discover your own as your path progresses. Create rituals that are meaningful to you.

Only you can be you. Trying to be someone else is not only futile, but robs the world of your beautiful gift, your song, your unique music. The esoteric teachings behind religious, spiritual and psychological systems are where the power resides.

The rosary, the Tibetan prayer wheel, the Ten Commandments/Words from the Torah, the Kabbalistic Tree of Life, Maslow's Hierarchy of Needs, the parables of Jesus, are all practices that point us inward. There is no magic in a bead or a prayer. The particular mode of prayer, contemplation or meditation is not what is important. It is the door that opens inward that matters.

Again, the Kingdom of God is *within*.

The biblical third commandment admonishes that we should not take the name of God in vain. Although the Hebrew people had many, many names of God, and Kabbalistic wisdom recognizes 72 Names of God, it is not the NAME that is holy. Each name represents a quality of the holy and is often unspoken. The belief is that the vibration of the name creates an entry point through which the seeker may go deeper to the Power and the Presence of God. Your true and authentic gift resides within you. When we "take the name of God within in vain" by ignoring the still small voice that is the calling of our deeper essence, we not only miss our own blessing, but we miss blessing the world.

The path of the Steps goes both inward and upward, and leads to enlightenment. It provides an inner rhythm and concrete tools for lifelong spiritual, mental, emotional, and physical growth.

THE STEPS

Because the 12-Steps are a developmental model of psycho-spiritual growth, they work in order, and some are grouped together. I have divided the developmental work into four stages:

Steps 1-3	The Foundation
Steps 4-7	The Inner Journey
Steps 8-9	Rectification
Steps 10-12	The Daily Walk

Once the entire cycle has been accomplished once, the use of tools from many Steps are beneficial and are part of the lifelong spiral journey inward. In general, once you are familiar with the process of Step work, you will be naturally inclined to follow the order of, for instance, looking within before making amends. The Steps become a way of life and as with any system, are practiced by the numbers to start and then become second nature.

THE GATEWAYS

The Gateways are a system of working the 12-Steps at a deeper level, combined with a principle, a Chakra, a color, musical vibration, gemstone, Chinese Meridian systems, and a suggested personal ritual for each level. There are more steps than Chakras, which honestly works just fine. By the time the later levels of outer/inner healing have been accomplished, a perfect system to integrate into the graph is the higher levels of Maslow's Hierarchy of Needs.

Each Gateway is a kind of portal into a deeper exploration of the spiritual principle of each of the 12-Steps and supports a lived spiritual practice. Here is how each Gateway is organized:

Essence of the Step | Chakra Functions and Physical Location | Sacred Geometric Shape
Color | Musical Note | Gemstone Therapy
Meridian | Gland | Ritual
Narrative Meditation on each Gateway

GATEWAYS 1-3
The Foundation

Clarity | Awakening | Relationship

Steps One through Three establish the foundation for the rest of the 12-Step work to follow. They are sometimes described as a three-legged stool. While each Step is distinct and very important, until each of the three has been engaged, a sufficient support for the inner journey of the 12-Steps isn't in place. Each Step leads into the next, but only after admitting powerlessness, coming to believe and making a decision are we ready to *move forward*.

GATEWAY ESSENCE 1
POWER

Step One: "Admitted we were powerless over ___, that our lives had become unmanageable."

Chakra . . . . Muladhara/ Root
Functions . . . . Safety, Grounding, Right to Live
Location . . . . Base of Spine
Sacred Geometric Shape . . . Upside Down triangle
Color . . . . Red
Musical Note . . . . Middle C
Gemstone Therapy . . . . . . Red Jasper
Meridian . . . . Circulation/ Sex and Large Intestine
Gland . . . . Adrenal
Ritual . . . . Color Infusion

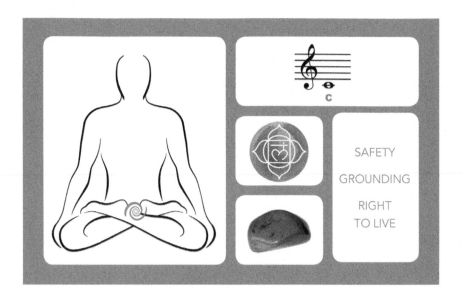

SAFETY

GROUNDING

RIGHT TO LIVE

Gateway 1 is about hitting bottom and discovering that instead of being the end of everything, it is the beginning of a whole new adventure.

No matter how hard we try to avoid it, at some point in our life's journey, we discover that our own will is not enough to fuel us. We lose a family member, endure a career disappointment, discover we have been betrayed or worse, and find ourselves in a desert of depression, despair or inertia.

This Gateway is about POWER. Bookshelves are full of titles about it. From political scientists to feminist scholars to gurus and self-help experts, the topic fascinates. We all need power!

Political scientists talk about structural power, feminist scholars explore power over versus power with. Preachers tell us about the power of prayer and mystics direct us to the power within.

The First Step is about power too – "LACK of power, that is our dilemma. We admitted we were powerless over (fill in the blank), that our lives had become unmanageable."

Once we have tried chemical power, personality power, money and success power and even star power, it is a huge relief to let go of the struggle, and allow a higher power to take over. It has been breathing us anyway, and making the trees grow and the tides go in and out. Once we admit that we are powerless over attempting to run the Universe, we discover that there is actually power in powerlessness!

To be honest, any activity we have to fortify with jet fuel (alcohol, cocaine, crystal meth, addictive sex, drugs, anger, sugar etc.) MAY not be the way to go. This is the Step where we finally stop and admit to ourselves that we are exhausted, and that on our own we are probably not making the best choices. We are...powerless over the drugs, chemicals, relationships and processes we have tried to use instead of God power. We are out of good ideas, and if we keep trying to push the river, we will only end up more defeated.

Someone once said it this way: "If you are wondering what God's will is for your life, and you feel like you are hitting yourself in the head with a hammer repeatedly, that's not it!"

Step One says, "Our lives had become unmanageable," and this is, we think, an understatement. It is time to let go. Sometimes we let go willingly, more often it is thrust upon us by circumstance, but however we reach this moment, the freedom that follows is Universal.

This is the bottom if we let it be. There can be lower lows, but if we get it that this bottom is as low as we want to go, an amazing thing happens. Once admitted, this bottom, this moment of powerlessness turns into a springboard- like a trampoline- that bounces us into a whole new way of life.

One thing is sure. We need a vision that

> "Lack of Power, that was our dilemma."
>
> -(ALCOHOLICS ANONYMOUS, CHAPTER 4-WE AGNOSTICS)

is bigger than our imaginations have come up with. We need a God sized vision, and the way we catch that is to listen. There are actually numerous techniques for visioning, but listening is part of all of them.

The idea of any vision quest is to stop and listen so we can hear the still, small voice within so we can catch the wave instead of fighting it. Whatever visioning process we use, the idea is to get into the flow, where we miraculously discover that a way has been prepared for us! Like finding ourselves on the freeway in an airstream behind a big truck, we are pulled rather than being the pusher. Ahhhhhh…

The paradox is that in finally letting go of our attempts to BE the generating power, we actually tap into a much greater power source. And since you are the only conduit for your unique and perfect gift, it is actually a relief to discover that you are not its Source. The Source of all creation flows through us and through all living things.

Chinese medicine calls this life force Chi. The Abrahamic traditions call it the Holy Spirit or Ruach/ Breath of God. Whatever we call it, our choice is not whether to access it, but rather when and how. Spiritual conversion is what some call this process, and it is about changing power sources. We need to reconnect to the grid! And since ultimately all lasting power comes from the Source of all creation, that is where we need to plug in.

One of the best known conversion stories is told in the biblical book of Acts 9: 1-20. Saul of Tarsus, a Greek educated Roman Jew, was among the most zealous defenders of what he thought was the one true way of the Torah. The problem wasn't with the Torah though, but with the interpretation of it by the Temple elite high priests, who were in collusion with the Roman Empire in oppressing the faithful. A very few people controlled all of the wealth and many observant Jews simply complied and paid their taxes and temple dues in order to avoid conflict.

The teachings of Jesus, once internalized, are liberating. After his death, many small communities or Jesus movements flourished, and although they were all very different from one another they all endeavored to follow the "Inner Way" and that made them less controllable. The Temple purists wanted these people gone.

As the story goes, one day on the road to Damascus on a mission of terror, Saul was literally struck blind and heard a voice that identified itself as Jesus. A series of miraculous interventions followed that dramatically altered the course of his life forever.

In a vision, God directs a man named Ananias, a follower of the Way, to pray with Saul. But Ananias is understandably reluctant to visit a notorious killer. He is however, obedient to the inner calling, lays hands on Saul, and "immediately something like scales fell from Saul's eyes, and his sight was restored." After this powerful turn of events, Saul became Paul, a zealous teacher of the path he had so virulently opposed. This is a dramatic awakening, to be sure, and Paul seems to have some personality issues whatever path he was following, but the story is a classic example of the conversion process. "Picked me up, turned me 'round, set my feet on solid ground" is the way an old song says it.

Here is the good news...

The biblical Saul was on a loser's path, but he thought he was serving a higher calling. God saw Saul's heart, and turned all of that misdirected energy into something constructive and transformational. He had to knock him over and strike him blind to do it, but the point was made and a whole new life of purpose began.

When we finally hit bottom, the good news is that there is always a backup power generator waiting! And this one has unlimited power. By the way, it was always there, but until the "scales are removed" from our eyes, we can't see too well.

The first three Gateways have to do with creating a solid foundation, a three-legged stool that doesn't wobble. They also resonate with hot colors Red, Orange and Yellow. In preparing your altar for the first three rituals, these colors will be a powerful enhancement of the vibratory power with which you will be aligning.

RITUAL FOR POWER

On your altar, arrange elements, photographs and symbols of the natural world.

Contemplate the bounty of nature, the vastness of the Universe. Now reflect upon your place in that cosmos.

Breathe deeply as you give thanks that you are part of a magnificent whole. You are not the genesis of the power of the Universe, but you are a crucial living component of it.

Red is a color that correlates with the root chakra.

The color red is an antidote to depression in Chinese medicine. Place red material or objects in places in your home where energy needs to increase or reconfigure. Breathe in the animating vibration of bright red; wear a red string around your wrist or neck. Connect to the power of the color red by placing red stones in a glass of water and placing it on a windowsill in the sun.

Allow the energizing properties of Red to infuse the water, and after at least five hours of infusion, drink the water.

Middle C is the musical note that resonates with the Root Chakra.

GATEWAY ESSENCE 2
PROCESS

Step Two: "Came to believe that a Power greater than ourselves could restore us to sanity."

Chakra . . . . Swadhisthana

Functions . . . . Emotions, Creativity, Sexuality

Location . . . . Lower Abdomen

Sacred Geometric Shape . . . Left Facing Crescent Moon

Color. . . . . Orange

Musical Note . . . . D and C#

Gemstone Therapy . . . . . . Goldstone and Carnelian

Meridian . . . . Bladder, Kidney, Large Intestine

Gland . . . . Testicles and Ovaries

Ritual . . . . Walking Meditation

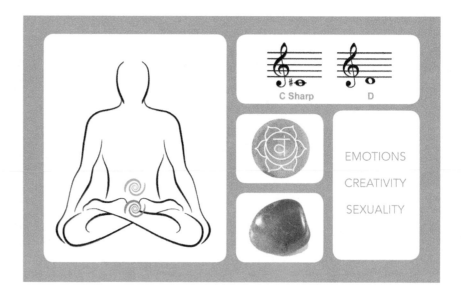

Waking up may be a one-time event, but awakening is a process. It has been said that negative stress is what happens when your mind resists what is. Our biggest problem in life may be our mind's resistance to life as it unfolds. Sometimes the answer is no, and unless we heed that, we are in for more pain.

Nature is a great teacher in this regard. Every seed doesn't flourish, every plant, or idea, doesn't make it. Nothing happens without process in the garden. Planting comes before blossoming, and blossoms break forth before the fruit. And another thing, you never get a rose bush if you plant a peach tree. Nature teaches us timing too. A bulb lives underground for many months, developing roots and storing up power for the big push through the crust of the earth in the spring. It sometimes seems like there is just no life there at all. But the Daffodil or Tulip or Sweet Hyacinth knows its own timing. It is the same way with people.

In Step One we stop hitting our head against the brick wall. We suddenly get it that surrender is the wisest choice. But "Surrender to WHAT?" That is the question of Step Two.

We come to believe that a power greater than ourselves can restore us to sanity. We surrender to the process that is running the universe, and little by little, we begin to trust that process.

What God do you believe in? Success, power, career, and self-will are popular gods with limited power. They will always let us down eventually, if we think they are our higher power. We *should expect* success, and love and creativity in our lives, and these are often components of a life well lived, but they are not God.

Another popular image of God is that of a punishing guy with a temper issue. Surrendering to that power would be an insane and self-destructive act. So it is at this point that it makes sense to look at the nature of a loving force for good as God.

The mystics tell us that God is vibration. So are we. As vibrational beings, we need to get into alignment with the Sound of All Creation, or OM, in order to resonate with the music of the spheres.

We do that by "coming to believe." Some tools for the reconnection include affirmative prayer, meditation, chanting, sacred service, and many forms of Body/Mind/Spirit healing. This higher power is not a function of our own self-will, but is the Source of all creation. It gives life, renews our strength, heals, transforms, was never born, never dies and once contacted doesn't leave us running on empty.

Dr. Nona Brooks of Divine Science says it this way: "God is everywhere. Therefore God is here. God is All, both visible and invisible."

In practicing this 2nd Gateway, we open to a flow of new life and creativity, harmonize polarities like up/down, right/left, in/out, male/female, and find balance. We get back into alignment with our inner essence, with our Creator, and with the world around us. Process, awakening, step by step, we begin to hear and feel and recognize our oneness with the Om – the Universal Sound. Yoga, Tai Chi, Alexander and Ayurveda, are all useful tools for accessing this coming to believe.

The story of the enlightenment of Siddhartha, or Gautama Buddha is also one of coming to believe. Born at least 500 years before the birth of Jesus, Gautama Buddha had a supernaturally blessed birth and a privileged, royal childhood. As the story goes, he never saw suffering or pain. But at the age of 29, he asked to leave the rarified environment of the palace, and when he did, he was shocked to encounter the existence of death and terrible suffering in the world. Gautama Buddha tried to change what he saw, to explain it, and finally, he sat down under a tree, a Bodhi Tree, and vowed to stay there until he could understand it. He was there for quite awhile, and ultimately emerged vowing to reincarnate lifetime after lifetime until human suffering is eradicated. This vow, known as The Bodhisattva Vow is a tall order. But the point, as it pertains to Gateway Two, is that sometimes we just need to do nothing, but stand there.

RITUAL FOR PROCESS-WALKING MEDITATION/ MINDFULNESS MEDITATION.

Preparation:

Surround yourself with the color orange. Put a fresh orange in a bowl. The vibration of the color orange has a property inherent in it that will stimulate your lower abdomen and allow the creative flow of sexuality and creativity to begin to flow. The scents of Tangerine and Cedar wood also work with the orange vibration to activate the physical willingness to begin the process of healing.

Sit in a sound bath of D and C#, even by playing the notes on a keyboard.

Choose a spot in nature if you can, but any-place will do. The quality of the inner journey is the point of this Ritual. For five minutes walk slowly, being mindful of each step, each breath, each element around you.

End your mindful walk with thanks for the power of the process of each moment.

Write for several minutes following your mindfulness walk, about your realizations.

End with thank you, and eat the orange if you want.

You are now ready to move forward.

GATEWAY ESSENCE 3
THE POWER OF YES

Step Three: "Made a decision to turn our will and our lives over to the care of God as we understand God."

Chakra . . . . Manipura/Nabhi
Functions . . . . Will, Social Self, Power to Act
Location . . . . Solar Plexus
Sacred Geometry Shape . . . . Upside Down Red Edged Triangle
Color . . . . Yellow
Musical Note . . . . E and E Flat
Gemstone Therapy . . . . . . Tigers Eye, Citrine, Amber
Meridian . . . . Stomach, Spleen, Small Intestine, Gall Bladder, Liver
Glands . . . . Pancreas, Liver
Ritual . . . . Water Ritual

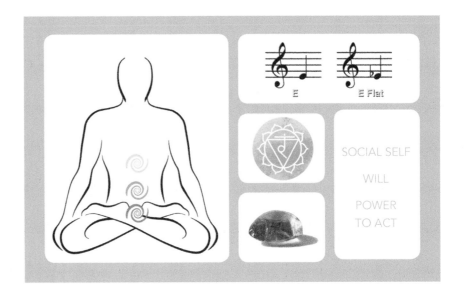

Are you prepared to endure the withdrawal from old habits? This is the question that comes with this stage of development. What is your answer? Are you ready to commit to your own transformation? "Is you is, or is you ain't?" is the way some folks say it. And Step Three is where we finally decide.

This is a Step of Surrender, a relinquishing of self-will and a decision to re-join the flow of the Universal OM. When we are experiencing the need to go deeper or go mad, we will say yes to almost any source of relief. But not just any source of relief will work. We have already tried that road.

In the early days of AA, very few people managed to access sobriety early in life. The two men who somehow reached out to one another across the void of despair and chronic alcoholism, fell upon a universal key to transformation. The key is that there is more healing power in one suffering person reaching out to another in true fellowship, than in all of the formal medical intervention in the world. These two men, one stockbroker on a business trip from New York City to Akron, Ohio, and the other a physician in Akron who was a chronic depressive hopeless alcoholic and much beloved wounded healer, found this key because each of them was in some way willing to make the decision to ask the Universe for help. And they were totally out of good ideas.

The essence of this healing moment is found in a picture of one hand reaching out to another. It is not a hand reaching down from above, to pull a person up, it is one person reaching out laterally. It is a moment of God reaching out to God.

So, "Is you is, or is you ain't?"

You have reached the decision point in the Hero's Journey. The decision is whether to embark or not embark. Do you want to be made whole? Looking back means the old familiar pain, and looking forward is the unknown. But there is another direction to look-Inward. Remember, the Kingdom of God is within. The power of choice is within.

Willing surrender of human limitation in Gateway One leads to coming to believe in a higher power in Gateway Two, followed by the process of becoming willing. And now we are at the doorway of deciding.

The Power of Yes correlates with the third chakra, with the color Yellow.

Musical notes E and E flat. The visual form of this chakra is an upside down triangle edged in red, in the Yellow field, surrounded by a ten-pointed flower.

This third chakra's influence fits perfectly with the Gateway Essence of Yes, as it influences self-esteem, warrior energy, and the power of transformation, and correlates with the Solar Plexus – the point of volitional power. So it is all about *choosing! There is a power in Yes!*

RITUAL FOR POWER OF YES

Water Ritual has been a part of sacred observances since the beginning of recorded history.

Submerging in a pool of water, and coming forth brand new is a powerful symbolic act and one that has a transformational effect.

Pouring of Libation to the Ancestors, Baptism

A libation is a ritual pouring of a liquid as an offering to call forth God or Spirit and the ancestors. Those who have transitioned from the physical realm dwell in the world of the ancestors. We honor them by summoning them forth, and bring them into our midst as supporters. Libation was common in many religions of antiquity and continues to be offered in many cultures today.

Various substances have been used for libations, most commonly water, wine or olive oil and in India, ghee – clarified butter. The vessels used in the ritual often have a significant form, which differentiates them from secular vessels (consecration). The libation can be poured onto something of sacred significance or into a potted plant or onto the earth.

Fill a pitcher or glass with water, and with reverence and the offering of a prayer, pour the water ceremonially into a plant, or onto the earth. The prayer should be one that honors the lineage from which you come, your ancestors, and the ancestors of your ancestors. In so doing, you summon the power of a deep connection to your endless lineage of support in the Invisible.

Baptism

The adoption of baptism in the Baptist church of the rural U.S. South by Africans brought to the United States against their will was a declaration of autonomy "hidden in plain sight." They were from many different countries in Africa, and spoke different languages but recognized the spirit of the Jesus teachings as that of the Trickster God, the shape shifting transcendent power. While the owners were trying to control with Christianity, the joyous worship of this living liberator gave life. And immersion in water was familiar as well, and held transformational power.

I would encourage you to consider removing your association of the practice with any particular formal religion, and to reclaim the practice as one of rejuvenation and rebirth.

Have a friend, a minister, a person you feel understands the depth journey, join you at a body of water, and participate with you in your ritual of rebirth.

You can wear a swimming suit or a white robe or nothing at all if you are in a secluded place. As you reflect upon the journey so far, and give thanks for your inner evolution, allow yourself to be dipped into the healing waters, and come up brand new. Close with a time of reflection, a shared meal with your friend, and give thanks.

{hug yourself}

LET'S GO IN!

There is a major difference between knowing the Steps and working the Steps. Think about attending a class and being handed a syllabus on the first day. You are not taking the class by just reading the syllabus, and neither are you working the Steps by hearing them but not doing the work. This is especially true of Step-4. The difference between the quality of recovery in people who do and do not do Step Four is dramatic. This point in the process of going inward represents a *fulcrum*...

ful·crum
'fo͝olkrəm,'fəlkrəm/
noun: **fulcrum**; plural noun: **fulcra**; plural noun: **fulcrums**

- the point on which a lever rests or is supported and on which it pivots.
- a thing that plays a central or essential role in an activity, event, or situation; i.e. "research is the fulcrum of the academic community."

I encourage you to forge ahead. The best way to get where you are going is to get on with it, or as the poet said:
"To begin, begin."-William Wordsworth

GATEWAYS 4-7
The Inner Journey

Clearing | Cleansing | Releasing

Steps Four through Seven are action Steps that require introspection, discipline, readiness to move on, a profound humility in asking God to remove our shortcomings, and a willingness to release these character traits. Holistically, these Steps represent the practice of an inner ecology, sometimes described as: Uncover, Discover, Discard.

GATEWAY ESSENCE 4
COURAGE

Step Four: "Made a searching and fearless moral inventory of ourselves."

Chakra . . . . Anahata

Functions . . . . Compassion, Love, Integration

Location . . . . Chest

Sacred Geometry Shape . . . . Six Pointed Star

Color . . . . Green/ Pink

Musical Note . . . . F and F#

Gemstone Therapy . . . . . . Aventurine and Turquoise

Meridian . . . . Heart

Gland . . . . Thymus

Ritual . . . . Feng Shui

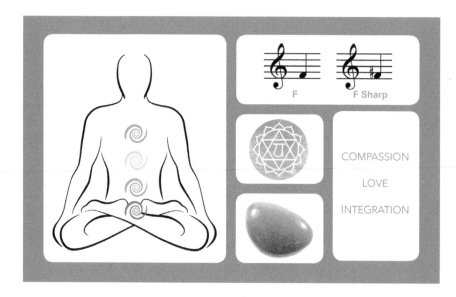

There can be a terrible consequence to the unexamined life. Suicide in the 35-64 year old range in the U.S. is up 26%, according to a 2015 survey. This is no joke. People are hurting. Step-4 takes us inside so that we can look at how we have blocked our gifts from coming forth, have hurt ourselves and others by acting out of fear, and begins the purge of the false self to make way for the true self.

If we do this inventory process thoroughly, "fearlessly and searchingly" as the Big Book says, we learn about ourselves, our motivations, and we also learn about our emotional triggers, and about the importance of being clear about our motives. And once we understand ourselves better, we can truly change destructive behaviors, and gain some compassion for ourselves.

"What you do not bring forth will destroy you," Jesus says. So this process is great for reversing self-destruction and opening a door to living in alignment with our higher selves. Until we have cleared away the years of shame, resentment, pain and fear, it is extremely difficult to access the inner essence of who we truly are meant to be.

We have got to go within. Eventually that is the only place left, and it was the original place anyway. We have to leave "home" to return home, to find home. It is that simple and that complicated.

Here are the four questions for the Step Four Inventory:

Who do I resent?
Why do I resent them?
What does it affect?
What did I do to perpetuate the pattern?

What this Step-4 process helps us do is to look at how we have become off base by trying to deal with resentment, loss and disappointment from a place of fear, with limited resources, and without the help of a higher power. No one shoots herself in the foot over and over again (the way addicts repeatedly do) if they feel happy,

"Nothing in life is to be feared, It is only to be understood."
-MARIE CURIE

"It was only later after allowing myself to bring forth what is in me, that I emerged not only as a leader, but as a Jedi Master."
-RETURN OF THE JEDI

"We shall not cease from exploration, and in the end of all our exploring we will arrive where we started and know the place for the first time."
-W.H. AUDEN

loved and secure. So this Step is about looking at our relationships and the way we have managed our insecurities.

Step-4 was created out of need. The original people in AA were thrilled to just be sober for a while, and after giving their struggle to a higher power, they felt great freedom…for a time. And then old memories began to come forward. Broken relationships and deep resentments were in front of their awareness.

Suddenly, they found themselves not in a good place, and it became critical to look at the world of resentments, to understand what had gone wrong, who they resented, why, and how they could get right with their pasts.

RITUAL FOR COURAGE – FENG SHUI

"There is a gift for us in each relationship that comes our way. Sometimes the gift is a behavior we're learning to acquire: detachment, self esteem, becoming confident enough to set a boundary, or owning our power in another way.

Some relationships trigger healing in us-healing from issues of the past or an issue we're facing today. Sometimes we find ourselves learning the most important lessons from the people we least expect to help us. Relationships may teach us about loving ourselves or someone else. Or maybe we'll learn to let others love us.

Sometimes, we aren't certain what lesson we're learning, especially while we're in the

midst of the process. But we can trust that the lesson and the gift are there. We don't have to control this process. We'll understand, when it's time. We can also trust that the gift is precisely what we need.

Today, I'll be grateful for all my relationships. I will open myself to the lesson and the gift from each person in my life. I will trust that I, too, am a gift in the other people's lives."

-Melodie Beatty

Feng Shui is both a gentle and powerful tool for establishing order, removing clutter, and clearing energy. An ancient Chinese philosophical system that means Wind-Water, Feng Shui is also described as the art of placement, and is so powerful that it can literally pop mirrors off of walls as the Chi, or living energy, begins to flow after an adjustment. The general idea is to create harmony with people and the surrounding environment.

Cleaning and rearranging your world can also involve relationship Feng Shui. All people come into our world for some reason. It is, however, a powerful tool to allow old assumptions about people to move along as well, as a part of restoring inner harmony.

There is also a related metaphysical theory called "The vacuum theory of prosperity." Nature cannot tolerate a vacuum, but we must take the responsibility for clearing out old ideas and identities, along with past guilt and pain, so that there is room for the new.

Holding shame inside causes inflammation

in the body and toxicity in the mind. Telling our secrets to a trusted other frees us from shame, guilt, regret and other causes of inflammation. Clearing physical and emotional clutter makes space for the movement of old hurts and resentments, and all energies that no longer serve us.

The Ritual for this step is to clean out one closet, drawer, file cabinet, garage, someplace where you have stored some kind of clutter. Choose one area, and commit to recycling anything from it that may be of value to someone else by taking them to the thrift store or recycling center. Have the courage to throw away papers, mementos, articles etc. that no longer are useful, and simply tie you to an earlier place.

Bless the process. Say thank you, as you begin to feel the renewed harmony of restored balance. Since nature cannot tolerate a vacuum, it is our job to create one periodically. If there is no room for the new and improved, we aren't available for increased flow. This 4th Step Ritual creates a vacuum that will now be ready to fill with re-directed purpose.

In recognition of the "emptying out" of our deepest regrets and areas of activity that have harmed us or others, we place upon our altar a bowl, a shell or a hollowed out gourd. As we reflect upon the "empty" space, we fill the bowl with flower petals, with beautiful shells, pinecones, and small crystals.

As we meditate for five minutes on the miracle of continual re-birth, we give thanks for renewed life more abundant.

Close this ritual with a blessing or prayer, and perhaps the sound of a singing bowl or gong to resonate in the new space we have opened.

GATEWAY ESSENCE 5
CLARITY

Step Five: "Shared with God, ourselves and another human being the exact nature of our wrongs."

Chakra . . . . Vishuddha

Functions . . . . Personal Truth, Expression, Etheric Energies

Location . . . . Throat

Sacred Geometry Shape . . . Om Symbol in Upside Down Triangle

Color . . . . Blue

Musical Note . . . . G and G#

Gemstone Therapy . . . . . . Blue Lace Agate and Sodalite

Meridian . . . . Lung

Gland . . . . Thyroid

Ritual . . . . Prism and Light

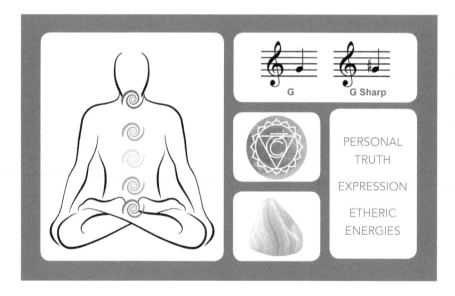

Step 5 has to do with understanding and assimilating what we have learned about ourselves through the process of inventory, and then clearing out the thought forms that are part of a former self. To share with God and with yourself is basically the same process, as you and God are one. However, denial can be pretty powerful and reminding ourselves about what we have admitted in Step Four is a good idea too. Then we have the luxury of letting it go by sharing our inventory with a trusted other. Some people choose a priest or minister, others a counselor or therapist. The idea is to choose someone who will have insight to offer, and will respect our confidence.

The Chakra for this Gateway is the Throat Chakra, and the color is blue. Because Steps Four and Five go together to complete a process of inventory and release, the green color and properties of the Heart Chakra are intermingled with the blue of the Throat Chakra. The heart chakra is particularly important because it is known as the transformer chakra. It transforms the lower survival energies, which can correlate with self-judgment and of others, into the higher vibration of compassion. So the loving but rigorous inner work of the heart combine with the telling of our secrets to a trusted other through the energies of the Throat Chakra.

This process of telling ourselves the real truth, of allowing our God self to lovingly receive that truth and then breaking free of isolation and shame by sharing our deeply held secret with at least one trusted other, opens us to true communion with God.

When we stop judging, we can begin loving, and allowing ourselves to be loved.

RITUAL FOR CLARITY

Place upon your altar a white candle, prism, a mirror and one small flower. Light the candle; place the prism and small flower on the mirror.

Meditate for several minutes on the principle of clarity, of perspective and the perfection of nature.

After several minutes, pick up the prism, and catch the light of the candle in its angles. Notice the rainbow colors reflected through the prism, and allow yourself to reflect upon the many properties of light.

Jesus taught that you are the Light of the world. If that light is obscured it cannot reflect the colors that are contained within its essence.

Close by giving thanks for a renewed clarity of vision.

GATEWAY ESSENCE 6
READINESS

Step Six: "Became entirely ready to have God remove these defects of character."

Chakra . . . . Ajna

Functions . . . . Wisdom, Transcendence, Universality

Location . . . . Forehead/ Third Eye

Sacred Geometry Shape . . . . Circle

Color . . . . Indigo

Musical Note . . . . A and B Flat

Gemstone Therapy . . . . Lapis Lazuli, Moonstone, Silver

Meridian . . . . Triple Warmer

Gland . . . . Pituitary

Ritual . . . . Troubling the Water

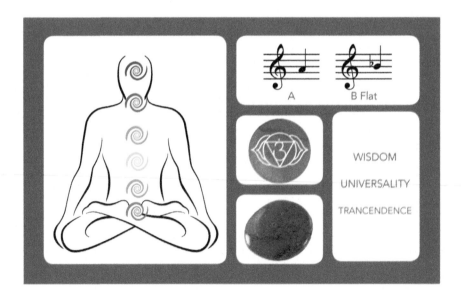

Being ready is something only we know for ourselves. We've asked and been asked thousands of readiness questions: Are you ready to leave? Are you ready to go onstage? Are you ready to run the marathon? Are you ready for the exam?

One of the really irritating things about a spiritual path is that sometimes it requires us to stand still until the next step becomes clear. It feels wonderful to be on a roll, and even in the case of letting go of false beliefs about who we are, there is almost a euphoria involved. But this Step is one that requires just becoming ready. It requires waiting, making both time and space for the insights we now have room to assimilate. Through the thorough and fearless Inventory of Step Four, and the process of sharing our innermost selves with another, we have essentially become rearranged at the cellular level. And even though it is extremely tempting to want to rush into asking God to remove the character traits about which we have felt shame or terrible discomfort, the wisdom of this Step is in waiting, and in becoming ready. This is a step all its own, and while the process does not have to be a long one, it seems that a pause is necessary for lasting change to really be established. The molecules need to rearrange. So we slow down, reflecting, praying, walking on the beach or howling to the moon, but not acting until we get the inner signal that we have reached a state of stability in our new lighter self, and are ready to move on.

The Old Testament Book of Psalms is part of the Wisdom genre of literature. There are numerous references to this idea of waiting and readiness in that book, but my favorite is, "Wait on the Lord, be of good courage and He shall strengthen your heart. Wait, I say, on the Lord."

RITUAL FOR READINESS

The phrase about God troubling the water has a Southern flare and a biblical origin. The reference is most often used in reference to the wonderful story of the healing fountain at Bethesda, "An angel went down and troubled the water…" John 5:4. The idea here is that this supernatural changing of the status quo holds the power of a paradigm shift, the gentleness of an angel's breath and the ability to move mountains of blocked energy.

For this ritual you will need a CD or an Mp3 of flute music, preferably a Native American solo. You will also need a bowl of water, some pebbles or a small round stone, and a mat on which to place the bowl, and a candle scented, preferably a blue one.

Water is a wonderful medium to use in contemplating the idea of both stillness and readiness. Flute music is used in the Native American tradition to open an energetic pathway into the realm of the Creator, so it is the perfect sound environment to prepare your spirit for this ritual.

> "God's gonna trouble the water…"
> NEGRO SPIRITUAL

65

You will be vibrationally prepared to receive the wisdom and cleansing power of the emptying steps you have undertaken through Steps Four and Five. As you bathe in the flute sound, fill a pretty bowl halfway with water. Place the bowl on a mat that complements it, and reflect upon the stillness in the water. Let the music infuse the water with receptivity. Then drop a small pebble into the bowl. Reflect upon the movement in the water that the stone creates. Listen to the sound of the music, breathe in and out with intention, and allow the stillness and conversely, the movement of the "troubled water" to connect you to the deep subconscious, to the realm where the Infinite abides.

Repeat the troubling as often as you wish, and contemplate your Oneness with the All that is. Ask in this dancing liminal zone if you are ready to move on. The answer will come.

When you hear the inner Yes, give thanks for your bravery and agency, for the completion of the emptying phase, and for the ever presence of Spirit in your life. Blow out the candle. Allow your elements of the in-between to remain on your altar for as long as they hold energy. Then clear your altar and prepare to move forward.

GATEWAY ESSENCE 7
RELEASE

Step Seven: "Humbly asked God to remove these defects of character."

Chakra . . . . Ajna

Functions . . . . Wisdom, Transcendence, Universality

Location . . . . Forehead/ Third Eye

Sacred Geometry Shape . . . Circle

Color . . . . Indigo

Musical Note . . . . A and B Flat

Gemstone Therapy . . . . . . Lapis Lazuli, Moonstone, Silver

Meridian . . . . Triple Warmer

Gland . . . . Pituitary

Ritual . . . . Dia de los Muertos

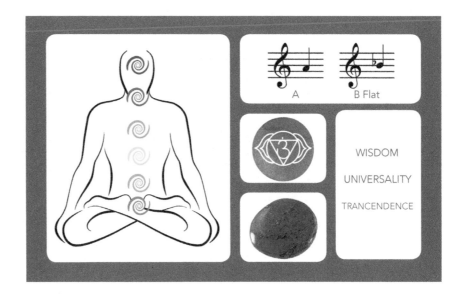

The two essences of Readiness and Releasing build upon one another. This is one of the places in the language of the original 12-Step materials where the fundamentalism of Dr. Bob crept in. Fundamentalist religions of many cultures have drawn a sharp line between good and evil, and have branded anyone who is perceived to be coloring outside the lines as defective, rather than creative.

In the original version it says, "We humbly asked Him to move all these defects of character." This is a problem. This language is a problem. It suggests that God is a man, and that something is inherently wrong with the person, rather than something about their behavior being counterproductive or missing the mark. Actually, this attitude is one of the things that can drive people away from recovery. We already feel defective, and filled with remorse too, by the time we get to these steps.

In any case, the idea here is that after we have completed a 4th and 5th Step, we should have a pretty good idea of how we habitually react to fear, and in so doing hurt others and ourselves. So these two steps are about looking at ourselves more clearly and deciding if we are ready to change.

A lot of us have split off parts of our personalities. We have called one part "good" and tried to hide the "bad," even from ourselves. This is a confusing way to live, and doesn't work very well without some addictive fuel. Integrative healing means just that…we integrate the parts of ourselves into a whole.

The Shadow Self is one way psychologists have described the aspects of our personalities that exists under the level of consciousness, and carries what our conscious mind may perceive as unacceptable traits. Sigmund Freud thought everything was about repressed sexuality, but his student Carl Jung, understood the unconscious mind to be operating at two different levels: the unconscious personal level, or Shadow, and the deep archetypal, or Collective Unconscious. Today we understand what Jung, poets and mystics have intuited for a long time, that we are connected to one another at a deep level. Physicists call it the quantum field, Chief Seattle calls it the web.

If we are unaware of our deeper levels of consciousness, this Shadow self can wreak havoc. Repressed longings eventually insist on being heard, and sometimes erupt when we are under the influence of some inhibition releasing substance. This is why integrative healing becomes important.

Step Six is about readiness and Step Seven letting go. We reintegrate, look at false personas and behaviors that have not served us, and ask to have them removed. This decision may be harder than you

> "I Release and I let go, I let the Spirit run my life, and my heart is open wide, yes, I'm only here for God."
>
> -RICKIE BYERS BECKWITH

think. We can get really attached to the familiar. What we are doing now is literally reintegrating parts of ourselves that we may not have realized were there. We are literally "re-membering." We actually think we *are* our old behaviors sometimes!

If you are hanging onto a judgmental, punishing God with an anger problem, this is a great time to re-think that. The God of the biblical prophets, the liberator God, who has always got your back, is a good one to access for this task.

Here is what that God promises us, through the prophet Jeremiah: "I know the plans I have for you. Plans to prosper you and not to harm you, plans to give you hope and a future" Jeremiah 29:1 Hebrew Bible. It's safe to release your shortcomings to that God, right? Let them go. Trust that there is good out there for you. Humbly ask.

Congratulations. You are more than halfway into a new life of the Spirit.

SEVENTH STEP PRAYER

"My Creator, I am now willing that you should have all of me, good and bad. I pray that you now remove from me every single defect of character, which stands in the way of my usefulness to you and my fellows. Grant me strength, as I go out from here, to do your bidding. Amen"

Page 76-Alcoholics Anonymous

RITUAL FOR RELEASE – DIA DE LOS MUERTOS ALTAR
Creating an Altar to the Ancestors

The Mexican holiday of Dia De los Muertos, or Day of the Dead is celebrated throughout Mexico and around the world in other cultures. The holiday focuses on gatherings of family and friends to pray for and remember friends and family members who have died. It is particularly celebrated in Mexico, where it is a national holiday, and all banks are closed. The celebration takes place on November 1 and 2, in connection with the Catholic holidays of All Saints' Day and All Souls' Day. Traditions connected with the holiday include the building of private altars honoring the deceased. Decorations often include sugar skulls, marigolds and the favorite foods and beverages of the departed. Many also visit the graves with these treats as gifts.

Scholars trace the origins of the modern Mexican holiday to indigenous observances dating back hundreds of years and to an Aztec festival dedicated to the goddess Mictecacihuati.

This holiday has spread throughout the world; in Brazil, *Dia de Finados* is a public holiday that many Brazilians celebrate by visiting cemeteries and churches. In Spain there are festivals and parades, and at the end of the day, people gather at cemeteries and pray for their dead loved ones. Similar observances occur elsewhere in Europe, and similarly themed celebrations appear in many Asian and African cultures.

Since we are letting go of character traits and behaviors that do not work for us, and by so doing are more deeply connecting to the other side, to the realm of the ancestors, the special ritual for this Step is an ancient traditional observance used in many cultures.

Create an altar to honor departed loved ones and invite them in prayer to join you there. Place upon your altar photographs of family, friends, animal companions who have passed on to the next dimension, along with marigolds, candles, figures of whimsically dressed skeletons, and things your ancestors enjoyed (and you may be letting go of) like booze, cigarettes, candy, or a favorite food. Play favorite music, dance favorite dances and share a meal with friends.

You are letting go of shortcomings that have held you in bondage but since they don't belong to your true self, there is also freedom as a result of the process. Enjoy constructing your altar and communing with the ancestors! There is humor and aesthetic pleasure in this ritual as well as deep power and symbolism. Leave the altar up for several days, living with the energies of past, present and future in this intermediate realm. You are a composite of all who have come before you, all you have been, and now you are opening into renewed life. Take time to rest and rejoice as you share a mini vacation with your ancestors.

By creating an altar to your ancestors, and maybe even to your former character traits, two things are accomplished. First of all, you honor the place of each of these moments and relationships in the becoming of who you are today. And secondly you prepare for the transition into a new life, by placing these relationships and character traits in perspective.

It is even possible to heal relatives and relationships with family members on the other side for both you and for them, through this ritual and during the process. When you deconstruct the altar, you will notice that you have the ancestral presence still with you. Your efforts on the behalf of your family system on both sides of the veil will be felt and appreciated.

Give thanks for your courage and willingness to undergo this inner work. Give thanks for God's breath breathing you.

Clear your altar and safely store the photos and objects that belong to your ancestors for future years.

Humbly ask God to remove all shortcomings and know that through this action, your prayer has been heard.

{ smile }

GATEWAYS 8-9
Rectification

Transition | Release

Steps Eight and Nine, once accomplished, represent the beginning of the end of isolation between us and our fellows. After doing focused inner work through the previous Steps, we know much more about ourselves, and are in a better position to know what wrongs we need to right. While we may be dying to apologize to people to get the heat off at earlier points in the 12-Step process, it is important to wait until after the previous Steps have been done thoroughly to make a list and begin formal amends. For instance, you may discover that you don't owe someone an amend at all once you work through the inner process of Inventory. But now is the time, and you are ready to clean up your side of the street.

GATEWAY ESSENCE 8
TRANSITION

Step Eight: "Made a list of all persons we have harmed and became willing to make amends to them all."

Chakra . . . . Sahasrara

Functions . . . . Enlightenment

Location . . . . Cerebral Cortex

Sacred Geometry Shape . . . Upside Down Violet Crescent

Color . . . . Violet

Musical Note . . . . B

Gemstone Therapy . . . . . . Amethyst

Meridian . . . . Central and Governing

Gland . . . . Pineal

Maslow's Hierarchy . . . . . . Basic

Ritual . . . . Zen Garden

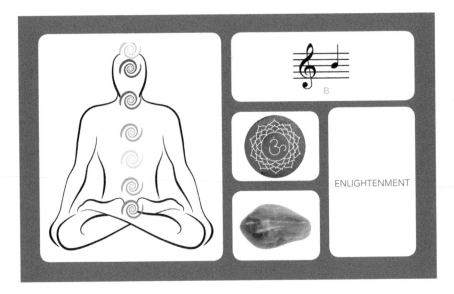

Step Eight is both a readiness step, and an action step. We make a list and become ready. The transformational work of the previous Steps is complete only when we make an honest attempt to right wrongs we may have caused. It may not be within our power to reconcile a situation, but it *is* within our power to make an honest attempt to clean up our side of the street. This Step, like Step 6, calls for both action and waiting. These are challenging and sometimes seemingly contradictory actions, but you are getting the hang of this paradox thing by now.

The list of all persons we have harmed is one we can write rather easily once we have completed Steps Four through Seven. We may discover that some people we thought we owed an amend do not belong on our list. It is important to wait until we know ourselves, and our motives, a little better before we decide who does and doesn't belong on this list. So now it is time to simply make the list and become willing.

Make a list.

Become willing.

RITUAL FOR TRANSITION

Both Step Eight and Nine are focused upon making amends.

Amend means to change. The Ritual for Step Eight has to do with restoring order.

A Zen garden is one in which each plant, stone, and design is placed with intention and

> "Hatred paralyzes life; love releases it. Hatred confuses life; love harmonizes it. Hatred darkens life; love illuminates it."
>
> -MARTIN LUTHER KING JR.

is a perfect metaphor for active, mindful focusing. You can create a small or large, indoor or outdoor Zen Garden with a shallow rectangular container or area filled with sand, and a rake to create designs in the sand. It is also typical to place stones in the design that can be moved each time you redesign the garden.

The purpose of a Zen Garden is different from normal yard work. It is an exercise in calming the mind and creating order. Decide what you wish to achieve by raking the Zen Garden each time you use it. Consider the pattern you would like to create and what it means to you in this moment. Take deep breaths while you are working to calm the body and mind. Use the opposite side of the rake to smooth sand and gravel. Stones; a soul stone, a body stone, can represent significant processes like transformation, past, present, future. Place the stones, or pile the stones as an integral element of your design.

Contemplate your garden.

Ask your deeper self if you have created a complete list for your amends.

When you receive confirmation, give thanks.

GATEWAY ESSENCE 9
RESTORATION

Step Nine: "Made amends to such persons except when to do so would injure them or others."

Chakra . . . . Sahasrara
Functions . . . . Enlightenment
Location . . . . Cerebral Cortex
Sacred Geometry Shape . . . Upside Down Violet Crescent
Color . . . . Cream
Musical Note . . . . B
Meridian . . . . Central and Governing
Gland . . . . Pineal
Maslow's Hierarchy . . . . . . Integration
Ritual . . . . The Vision Board

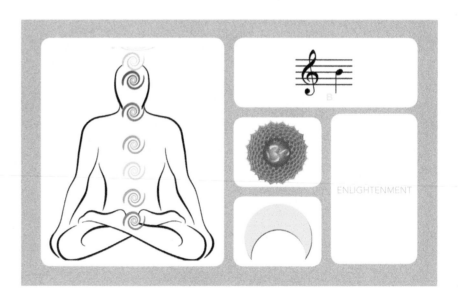

ENLIGHTENMENT

We have now begun a process through which true repair and forgiveness can begin. With each new level of the inward journey, we are becoming closer to a relationship of harmony with our Creator. Steps eight and nine are all about getting back into alignment with God.

In AA literature, there is great importance given to both Steps 8 and 9. We stand at a threshold. The practicing of these two Steps opens the door to "The beginning of the end of isolation." And that is a big deal.

You may have heard that "when the student is ready, the teacher appears." This seems to be the way with making amends too. By deciding who is and isn't on our amend list, we put a powerful intention into the Universe. There is no better example of how this idea of "as within, so without" works than the Ninth Step process. Remember, you will probably have done some depth work in Steps Four and Five on the reasons you have taken certain fear based actions in your relationships. Your choice of a trusted other to share the Fifth Step with will make a big difference too, as they will ask questions and share personal experiences that will open doors of insight for you. The idea here is not only to make an amend, but to begin to understand ourselves well enough that we will not be likely to repeat the same behaviors. So by the time you have become ready to make the amend, the opportunity often presents itself for you to speak with the person in question.

When you meet with them, remember that you are in a process of inner transformation, and you are approaching them in order to let them know that you are truly sorry, but also to free yourself from carrying the burden any longer. Some amends involve making financial restitution. Some involve a conversation. We can also right wrongs with people who are no longer in the physical by writing a letter. The point is that you are taking the time and setting the intention to right wrongs.

As you make these amends, you will be surprised about how much easier things become. It is at this point that the 12-Step literature assures us that we have reached the beginning of the end of isolation, know a new freedom and a new happiness, and will begin to understand the benefit of even your most painful experiences in helping another. The Promises, listed again below:

THE PROMISES

If we are painstaking about this stage of our development, we will be amazed before we are halfway through.

1. We will know a new freedom and a new happiness.
2. We will not regret the past, nor wish to shut the door on it.

"In God we live and move and have our being."

ACTS 17:28

3. We will comprehend the word serenity, and we will know peace.

4. No matter how far down the scale we have gone, we will see how our experience can benefit others.

5. That feeling of self-pity and uselessness will disappear.

6. We will lose interest in selfish things and gain interest in our fellows.

7. Self-seeking will slip away.

8. Our whole attitude and outlook upon life will change.

9. Fear of people and of economic insecurity will leave us.

10. We will intuitively know how to handle situations, which used to baffle us.

11. We will suddenly realize that God is doing for us what we could not do for ourselves.

Are these extravagant promises? We think not. They are being fulfilled among us – sometimes quickly sometimes slowly. They will always materialize if we work for them.

-Alcoholics Anonymous pg.83, 84-

AA World Services Inc.

RITUAL FOR RESTORATION- THE VISION BOARD

A vision board, also called a Treasure Map, is typically a poster board on which you paste or collage images you have torn from different magazines as a visual representation of who you want to become, where you want to live, where you want to go on vacation, etc. This is the perfect place in your journey inward to begin to create with intention, and visual images communicate directly with the subconscious mind. You can also draw pictures, add words and anything that represents what this newly emerging self will be. You have done some considerable interior rearrangement and purging of behaviors and identities that no longer serve. So dream big!

There are countless stories about the power of the Vision Board as a directive to the inner self. Some people have found themselves surprised to discover that they have manifested almost exact replicas of their Vision Board dream. The idea here is to create a visual inspiration that carries the feeling, tone, and energy of the life you envision. When you are happy with your creation, put the board in a place where it will serve as a visual prompt for your subconscious mind.

Don't forget that you will want to take things off and add things to the vision board as you change and grow.

Have fun! Give thanks. Moving on!!

{be still}

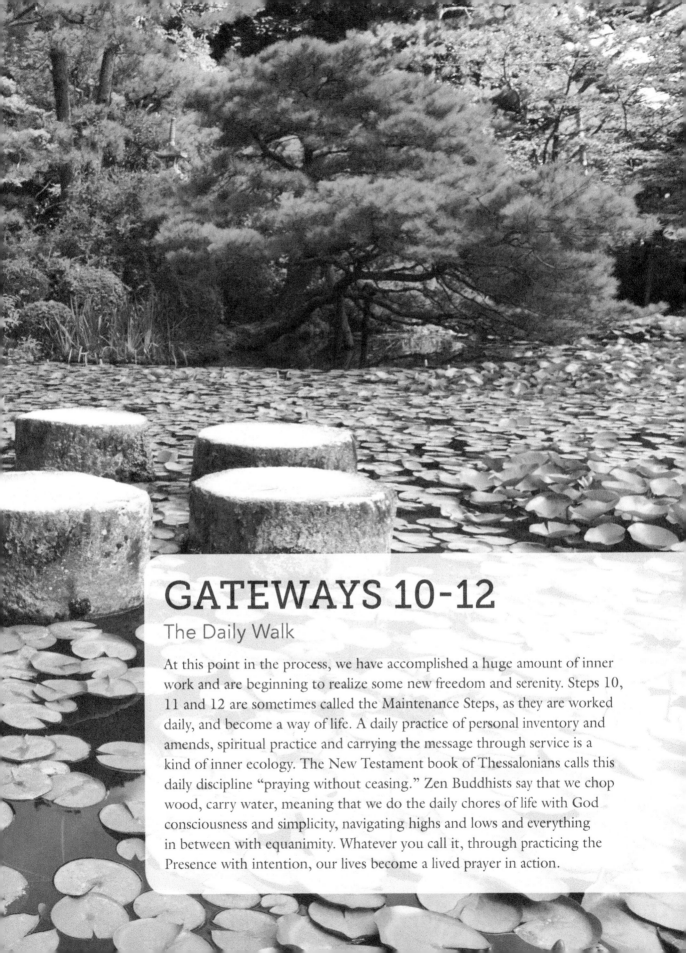

GATEWAYS 10-12

The Daily Walk

At this point in the process, we have accomplished a huge amount of inner work and are beginning to realize some new freedom and serenity. Steps 10, 11 and 12 are sometimes called the Maintenance Steps, as they are worked daily, and become a way of life. A daily practice of personal inventory and amends, spiritual practice and carrying the message through service is a kind of inner ecology. The New Testament book of Thessalonians calls this daily discipline "praying without ceasing." Zen Buddhists say that we chop wood, carry water, meaning that we do the daily chores of life with God consciousness and simplicity, navigating highs and lows and everything in between with equanimity. Whatever you call it, through practicing the Presence with intention, our lives become a lived prayer in action.

GATEWAY ESSENCE 10
PRACTICE

Step Ten: "Continued to take personal inventory and when we were wrong, promptly admitted it."

Chakra . . . . Anahata

Functions . . . . Compassion, Love, Integration

Location . . . . Ethereal/Energetic Body

Sacred Geometry Shape . . . Upside Down Crescent

Color . . . . Crystal

Musical Note . . . . F and F#, G and G#

Gemstone Therapy . . . . . . Clear Quartz and Aventurine

Meridian . . . . Heart

Gland . . . . Thymus

Maslow's Hierarchy . . . . . . Love and Psychological Integration

Ritual . . . . Feng Shui

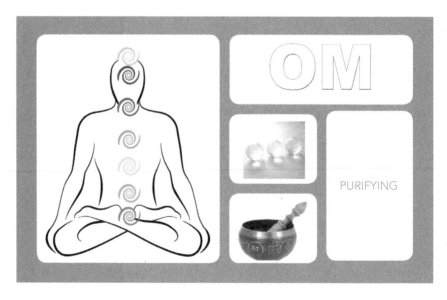

Once we have done the inner work of examining our life to date, the idea is for us to develop a daily practice that will sustain our gains, and prevent us from needing to do that depth of work again. We need a daily walk, a practice, a discipline. Developing a technique for returning to center in the midst of life's tumultuous storms is critical.

Step Ten is a daily practice of inventory as practiced more in depth in Steps 4 and 5 combined. The idea of working the Steps is to become self-aware enough to examine our behaviors at the end of each day and make amends promptly so that we don't build up a huge repository of resentments again. We need never repeat the 4th and 5th Step in full if we do a "thorough and fearless" inventory the first time around, and make a habit of taking personal inventory daily.

RITUAL FOR STEP 10

At the end of each day or any time during the day if you discover that you are upset or off balance, take a moment to reflect, to go inside. If there is any word or action that needs to be righted, you will know.

Write down anything that you may need to process more deeply.

Make note of the amend you want to make, or make it if possible.

At days end, give thanks, and close your eyes in sleep.

GATEWAY ESSENCE 11
ONENESS

Step Eleven: "Sought through prayer and meditation to improve our conscious contact with God as we understand God, praying only for knowledge of God's will for us and the power to carry it out."

Chakra . . . . Crystal Above Head
Functions . . . . Purifying
Location . . . . Ethereal/Energetic Body
Color . . . . Clear Quartz and/or Carnelian and Citrine
Musical Sound . . . . OM
Maslow's Hierarchy . . . . . . Self Actualization
Ritual . . . . Singing Bowl

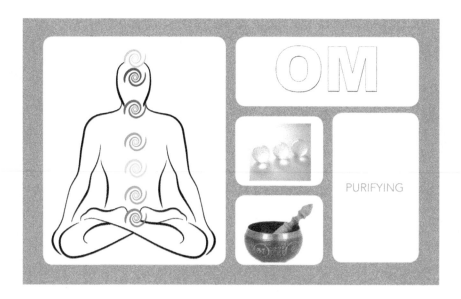

The word in this Step that calls out is "Sought." To seek means to go beyond one's present level of understanding and strike out into the unknown to look, in this case, for conscious contact with the Source of All Creation, and it suggests two effective tools for that search... prayer, and meditation. This journey is one that is inner.

Prayer is sometimes said to be talking to God and meditation listening to God. Really the processes are sides of the same coin.

PRAYER

There are as many ways to pray as there are to be human, but maybe the simplest prayer is "Help!" There is no right or wrong prayer as long as the prayer is focused on universal good. Holding a thought deep in your heart with intention is a prayer, so be aware of your thoughts!

The New Thought Tradition describes five basic steps to affirmative prayer:

1. There is One God
2. God is...(good, harmony, abundance, etc)
3. I am one with God
4. Thank you
5. Let Go and Let God/ Release

Prayer is one of the five pillars of Islam, and is performed five times a day in surrender to prayer, facing Mecca.

Chanting or reciting the Rosary is prayer, the use of Buddhist prayer beads and a prayer wheel, Sufi whirling and Buddhist chanting are all prayer, as are sailing on the ocean and contemplating the vastness of God. Try different things and your method will find you. Again, the point here is to pray ONLY for knowledge of God's will for us, and the power to carry that out.

MEDITATION

Meditation is a 'going within' to open us to the inner realm of the Infinite. Chanting and mindfulness meditation, chanting with or without a mantra, repetitive moving meditations like Tai Chi are all forms of meditation and connect us to the infinitely spacious inner realm. We now know that by choosing to be centered on the connection with the Infinite through a daily practice, changes our brains at the cellular level, calms stress and expands consciousness.

"When you have shut your doors, and darkened your room, Remember never to say that you are alone For you are not alone, but God is within, And your genius is within."

-EPICTETUS

Meditation is often focused on allowing thoughts to pass through the conscious mind without getting hooked by any one of them. Sometimes that is a lot easier said than done! The inside of our heads can be a pretty noisy place when we first go into the silence.

Contemplation is a form of meditation focusing on a thought or idea. Very kinesthetic, or action-oriented people sometimes do best with a moving repetitive practice like hot yoga or using a mantra, or both.

The Bento Box of Mind, Body Tools at the end of this book contains some other methods you might try as you seek the inner kingdom of God.

And when you seek, as Saint Thomas says…a magnificent journey begins.

RITUAL FOR ONENESS

The Singing Bowl, native to Tibet and Nepal, is used worldwide for meditation, music, relaxation and personal well-being. The bowl is actually a type of bell, specifically classified as a standing bell. Singing bowls come in many sizes and musical tones and materials. Pick one that works for you and resonates with peace at your deepest cellular level. Choose a time to focus on sounding the singing bell, as a way to clear energy in your space and internally.

There are many techniques for utilizing the bowl, but the best method for you will be discovered through practice. Listen to your own inner resonance with various sounds as you experiment.

Strike the singing bowl, and allow the tone to ring your being.

Enter the inner chamber through prayer, meditation, chanting or yoga daily.

Breathe.

Return to center.

Give thanks.

GATEWAY ESSENCE 12
SACRED SERVICE

Step Twelve: "Having had a spiritual awakening as the result of these steps, we shared the message with others and practiced these Principles in all of our affairs"

Chakra . . . . Crystal Above Head
Functions . . . . Purification, Activation of Etheric Light Field
Location . . . . Etheric/ Energetic Body
Color . . . . Clear Crystal and Turquoise
Musical Note . . . . OM
Maslow's Hierarchy . . . . . . Peak Experience-Enlightenment
Ritual . . . . Labyrinth

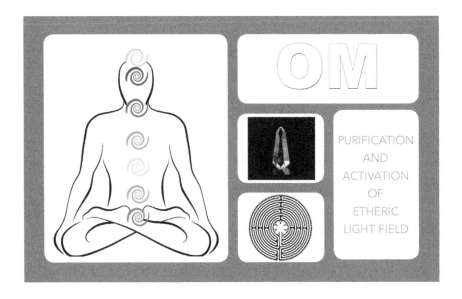

Once you have worked through the preceding Steps and Gateways, you will discover that to remain in the flow of Universal Oneness you must be of service. Life is constant change. We either are moving forward or backward, and the action of service assures that we are in the flow of the highest vibration. Numerous studies have shown that altruism, or selfless service, blesses the person or situation you serve, quickens the immune system, widens the worldview and becomes a way of life. You truly can't keep it unless you give it away. The good news is that there are a million ways to be of service to the world. The point here is action. Choose, act, do something that makes a positive difference in someone's life or in the world. Do something nice for someone and don't get found out.

Step Twelve states that *the* result of practicing the Steps is to have a spiritual awakening, and that once we wake up we need to share the message with others. It is really simple, not necessarily easy to be sure, but simple.

You can't keep it unless you give it away!

This reaching out to help another is the very essence of the 12-Steps. It is how and frankly, why they work.

THE SPIRAL PATH:

The ancients describe the spiral as a metaphorical symbol for understanding spiritual action or process. The spiral launches us with great energy, and then the thrust doubles back on itself before moving forward again. This doubling back is a time for shedding anything that is no longer of use. It is *critical* for us to shed, if we plan to move forward into life with light and authenticity. The Steps support this action perfectly, thrusting forward, doubling back for introspection and letting go, amending and repairing, reconnecting, serving and again thrusting forward.

RITUAL FOR SACRED SERVICE THE LABYRINTH

A labyrinth is an intricate maze in which it is a challenge to find the exit. The origin of the maze is in Greek mythology. The pattern is widely used to symbolize the journey of life, and can be a wonderful meditation on the twists and turns of the walk we embark upon each day. Running into dead ends, seemingly impassible cul-de-sacs and puzzling twists and turns, the persistent labyrinth walker will find the way out, in and through at the same time.

> "Inaction breeds doubt and fear.
> Action breeds confidence and courage.
> If you want to conquer fear, do not sit home and think about it.
> Go out and get busy."
>
> -DALE CARNEGIE

You are integrating, rooting and expanding;
Integrating your conscious and unconscious selves.
Rooting in good soil with the ancestors.
Expanding through service.
You are alive.
Breathe. Give thanks. Give it away.

> "The best way to find yourself is to lose yourself in the service of others."
>
> -MOHANDAS (MAHATMA) GANDHI

{breathe}

PUTTING IT TOGETHER
A TWELVE WEEK MODEL

The 12-Step Path is a "we" journey. While there is much individual inner work required of us as we progress through the Steps, we never have to do it alone.

If you decide you would like to gather people for a community spiritual event, the following is a template for a Twelve Week 12-Step Spiritual Program, with topics all drawing from reflection upon the 23rd Psalm. You can use this model or develop your own, integrating this text or one you love, and adding some of the tools that inspire you from the Gateways.

Psalm:23

"The Lord is my shepherd, I shall not want.
He maketh me to lie down in green pastures,
he leadeth me beside the still waters,
he restoreth my soul. He leadeth me in the
paths of righteousness for his name's sake.
Yay though I walk through the valley of the
shadow of death, I shall fear no evil,

for Thou art with me. Thy rod and thy staff
they comfort me.
Thou prepareth a table before me in the pres-
ence of my enemies,
Thou anointeth my head with oil, my cup
runneth over.
Surely goodness and mercy shall follow me all
the days of my life,
and I shall dwell in the house of the Lord
forever."

Suggested Outline for A 12-Step Spiritual Gathering with Discussion

- Introduce topic and share on your insights about it for 10-20 minutes.
- Enjoy Ritual of your choosing.
- Give thanks.
- Collect an offering to practice the law of circulation, and to honor the speaker with a gift, pay rent etc.

- Bless the offering, close with a group song or chant.

Suggested Meeting Topics

- 23rd Psalm – Who are my "enemies"?
- Who/What is your Higher Power? Victory through surrender.
- Confession/ 5th Step – Honesty – Sharing the load. My secrets are too heavy a burden to bear alone.
- "The bible tells me so." Just what is the bible and why might it be a tool for me to use today? Same question may be entertained about other wisdom texts.
- The Universe responds to a cheerful giver – The paradox: You can't keep it unless you give it away. Abundance and true prosperity flows from the Source of all creation, not from our jobs, parents. lovers, spouses. What is the Law of Reciprocity and how does it apply to this idea?
- How could this happen to me? When painful things happen to good people. Considering the Highest Perspective, God's view.
- Why were we chosen? God's special gift to recovering people.
- "You never get more than you can handle." Oh yeah? The heat feels like it might burn us up, but gold is refined in the hottest fire.
- Your Heart's Desire – God speaks to us through the still, small voice within.
- Footprints – "Where were you God?" "When you only saw one set of footprints in the sand, I was carrying you."
- Amazing Grace – Recovery is a true gift of grace. What we do with that gift determines whether we get to keep it.
- Does God love me just as I am, or do I have to pretend to be somebody's version of good to be ok with God? – Finding and learning to love our inner, unique, God given perfection.

The format for a service can be a simple one:
- Open with singing or instrumental music, with a call to worship on a singing bowl or chime.
- Greeting, followed by a five or ten minute meditation.
- Recitation of The Lord's Prayer from the Aramaic Translation, or some prayer of your choice.
- Musical selection/ poetry/ a dance piece/ some artistic offering.

"PICK A PATH – ANY PATH, AND GO DEEPER"
-PARAMAHANSA YOGANANDA

There are many paths...but only one destination. **The Path is Simple – the answer is YES!!!** The 12-Step path is a holistic, developmental model. The journey we have just embarked upon utilizes Gateways as entry points to combine the Steps with the Wisdom Path. We have explored the lived Jesus Path, the Way of the Tao, the Chakras and more. These represent a roadmap. The possibilities on the inward journey are myriad, but the road gets narrower as we progress.

Singer Erykah Badu describes a holistic spiritual path this way...I think you will like it:

"I subscribe to five doctors: Dr. Sun, making sure we get enough Vitamin D; Dr. Nutrition, making sure our vital bodies are clean and healthy, performing up to its highest ability;

Dr. Exercise, at least fifteen minutes a day; Dr. Spirit, making sure that you communicate with the highest part of yourself, the highest form that you can imagine; and Dr. You, making sure that you take time to take care of you."

Thank you and bless you for having the courage to change our world by doing your own inner work. When you change your consciousness from one of fear to one of love, you are healing the world too.

Go deeper and wider in your spiritual journey. Remember you always have the 12-Steps and the tools of each Gateway to return to as your orienting center.

{enjoy}

TOOLS FOR YOUR TRANSCULTURAL, INTER-SPIRITUAL BENTO BOX

Bento (弁当, bentō) is a single-portion takeout or home-packed meal common in Japanese cuisine. A traditional bentō holds rice, fish or meat, with pickled or cooked vegetables, usually in a box-shaped container. The containers and arrangements are often colorful and creative in presentation, mixing and matching different elements.

Like the beautiful art boxes of Ira Joel Haber,

Original Art by Ira Joel Haber

an Inter-spiritual, Inter-cultural Bento Box can be seen as a kind of Tool Kit for Body, Mind, Spirit practices.

The life of the Spirit is a bountiful feast, and as you become familiar with the basics of the 12 Steps and Gateways, you will find many ways to customize your own walk, by using some of the following ingredients. Have fun!

Remember, we are using the 12-Steps and the Gateways as the spine of the journey, so you will always have someplace to return to orient your Path inward.

AN INTER-SPIRITUAL HOLISTIC BENTO BOX OF TOOLS

BODY:

Organic diet, nutrition, herbs, exercise, massage, vitamins, fresh air, sacred sexuality, sufficient rest, yoga, dance, body-work of many kinds (Alexander, Rolfing), work with energy healers, color, light and auric awareness, recreation, laughter, dance, drumming, singing and music of all sorts, sports. We have to MOVE to be alive, and what we feed ourselves determines how alive we are. Organic food is alive, processed food is dead, and GMO's are alien DNA. Your goal is to ingest the living vibration for the nourishment of your living cells. We are what we eat.

The combination of yoga asanas and healing essential oils is a wonderful support for your journey.

Use the following sequence separately or as a full practice to unblock and balance Chakras.

ROOT CHAKRA:
YOGA POSE – TREE
ESSENTIAL OIL – PATCHOULI

SACRAL CHAKRA:
YOGA POSE – BUTTERFLY/COBRA
ESSENTIAL OIL – SANDALWOOD/YLANG YLANG

SOLAR PLEXUS CHAKRA:
YOGA POSE – BOW
ESSENTIAL OIL – CINNAMON

HEART CHAKRA:
YOGA POSE – CAMEL
ESSENTIAL OIL – ROSE

THROAT CHAKRA:
YOGA POSE – SUPPORTED SHOULDER STAND
ESSENTIAL OIL – EUCALYPTUS

THIRD EYE CHAKRA:
YOGA POSE – LOTUS
ESSENTIAL OIL – LAVENDER

CROWN CHAKRA:
YOGA POSE – SAVASANA
ESSENTIAL OIL – FRANKINCENSE

MIND/EMOTIONS:

Concrete tools: Communication skills, dynamics of communication in open as opposed to closed systems. Gestalt Therapy, Family Systems Therapy, Shadow work, Cognitive Behavioral Therapy, New Thought psycho-spiritual core teachings and practices, 12-Steps, *The Four Agreements*, Sacred poetry from many traditions – Rumi, Tao Te Ching, Qigong, Freud, Jung, Developmental Psychology, Maslow's Hierarchy of Needs, Philosophy, Anthropology, Metaphysics, Art, Art History, Applied Art, Science, Physics, Geometry, Gratitude, 12-Step meetings. You Are What You Think.

SPIRIT:

Practicing the Presence… Different in Different Cultures: Prayer, Meditation, Affirmations, Breath work, Observance of the Sabbath, Yoga, Silence, The Beach, Ritual, Depth Psychology, Music, Chanting, Working with a Guru/Rabbi/Teacher, Making Art, Engaging with nature, Color, Line, Design, Harmony, Study of Torah, Bible, Course in Miracles, Tao Te Ch'ing, Koran, Bhagavad Gita, Upanishads, Koran, and other sacred texts.

RITUAL:

Ritual is an outer observance that anchors the sacred in our hearts. Ritual silently signifies identity to our deepest subconscious mind as well as to the outside world.

Recitation of the Sh'ma "It shall be a matter of writing it on your heart, of holding it in your mind, with all of your might"

Praying five times a day, communion, baptism, singing sacred music, common prayer, recitation of the rosary, chanting, rhythmic whirling, and Ecstatic journeying are all forms of prayer.

You will discover what rituals resonate with your deep soul path.

The practice of these tools can be understood as more homeopathic than allopathic. Homeopathy distills the power of a cure from the essence of the illness it seeks to minimize. The homeopathic Gateways open inward and connect us to the root of separateness from our highest nature, and allow us to stimulate that root so it can serve as the springboard for a transformational spiritual awakening.

• • •

You will see in the core tenants of the paths below that truly, "One Spirit Many Expressions" is the essence of the wisdom path.

The Jesus Path

- The Kingdom of God is within
- Seek and you shall find
- Love one another
- Take care of "the least of these"

10 Words or Commandments of the Torah

- I am the Lord thy God
  Thou shall have no other Gods before me
- No graven images or likenesses
- Do not take the Lord's name in vain
- Remember the Sabbath Day
- Honor thy father and mother
- Thou shall not kill
- Thou shall not commit adultery
- Thou shall not steal
- Thou shall not bear false witness
- Thou shall not covet

Hindu Four Ways to God

- **Jnana Yoga** Way of Knowledge
- **Bhakti Yoga** Single pointed devotion to love of God
- **Karma Yoga** actual work in form of service
- **Raja Yoga** Royal Way-physical exercises and psychological practices; pranayama, tantra, Samadhi

10 Sacred Laws of Native American Spirituality

- The Earth is our Mother, care for her
- Honor All Your Relations
- Open your heart and soul to the Great Spirit
- All life is sacred; treat all beings with respect
- Take from the earth what is needed and nothing more
- Do what needs to be done for the good of all
- Give constant thanks to the Great Spirit for each day
- Speak the truth, but only for the good for others
- Follow the rhythms of Nature
- Enjoy life's journey but leave no tracks

Five Pillars of Islam

- Shahadah-Profession of faith
- Salah-Ritual Prayer
- Zakat-Almsgiving
- Sawm-Fasting
- Hajj-Pilgrimage

Eightfold Path of Buddhism Bodhisattva Vow

- **Right View** To see and understand things as they really are
- **Right Action** Mental action that controls our actions
- **Right Speech** First principle of ethical conduct
- **Right Action** 2nd principle of ethical conduct
- **Right Livelihood** Purpose driven work
- **Right Effort** Discipline
- **Right Mindfulness** Controlled and perfected faculty of connection
- **Right Concentration** One pointedness of mind

FENG SHUI:

The art of Feng Shui we hear about most frequently originated in China. Wind and Water is the literal translation of the words, and the practice is designed to bring harmony among the elements of Air, Earth, Water and Fire, within the home. Ancient cultures other than China have versions of this practice of connecting nature and our lived environment, and beyond any cultural understanding, our souls long for balance and harmony in our surroundings.

Mythologist Joseph Campbell explains it this way:

"To live in a sacred space is to live in a symbolic environment where spiritual life is possible, where everything around you speaks of the exaltation of the spirit. This is a place where you can simply experience and bring forth what you are and what you might be. This is the place of creative incubation. At first you might find that nothing happens there. But if you have a sacred place and use it, something will eventually happen. Your sacred space is where you find yourself again and again."

-Joseph Campbell, The Power of Myth

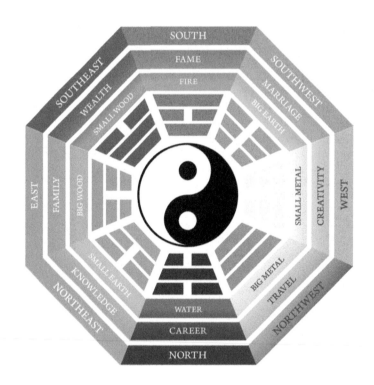

SACRED GEOMETRY:

Sacred geometry is a kind of geometry used in the design and construction of religious structures from cathedrals to yurts. The way I am using the term has to do with building an inner sacred scaffolding to support the journey inward and back to self and upward to enlightenment. It is good for us to be aware of shapes and forms in the unseen.

Sacred geometry appears in many wisdom teachings, like the biblical story of Jacob's ladder in which Jacob dreams about a stairway to heaven with angels ascending and descending. This stairway is also the origin of the Kabbalistic Tree of Life. I have found that by envisioning and building a structure to support my own inner path, I have someplace visual to return when I need to touch base. Each stairway goes both higher and deeper and ultimately leads to union with the Source.

The diagram below is called The Flower of Life. It is a universal symbol found in architecture and literature all around the world. It is said to contain all of the patterns of Creation.

HEALING THE ETHERIC BODY:

All transformational healing is multidimensional. The trick is to integrate mind, body, spirit and soul while remembering our essential wholeness. Mystics, swamis, rabbis, gurus, ministers, shamans, yogis and wise ones of the ages have taught that there are layers of energy in living things, beyond the gross physical. The etheric body, aura, or energy field emanates from the physical body, and can even be seen with the eye by energy sensitive people.

You have consciously felt a person's energy without actually seeing them first at some time or another, right? You may be sitting in a room and suddenly are aware that you aren't alone, and when you turn around you can see that someone is looking at you or has wordlessly entered your energetic field, right? You also know the feeling of sensing something about a person that doesn't go along with their words. You may have even said, "I just don't like his vibe," right? Ralph Waldo Emerson speaks to this when he observes, "Who you *are* is yelling so loud, I can't hear what you *say* to the contrary!"

Yogis call this energy field that speaks loudly but wordlessly, our etheric body. It is the field that Reiki masters like Jesus of Nazareth worked in to create miraculous healings. In order for our bodies to fully heal, we have to address wounds in the etheric body. Along with holding vibrations and colors, the etheric body holds unhealed trauma too. Eckhart Tolle calls this trauma layer the "pain body." Extreme stress and addiction can create holes in the etheric body that leave us open to illness or psychic attack. We block our deeper sensitivities when we are under the effect of a mood changing substance, and open ourselves to unwanted energies. So when we enter the 12-Step healing journey, we not only need to heal the physical and psychological bodies of ourselves, but our etheric/energy body too. You may have seen or experienced a Reiki master working with energies this way. The Reiki master's touching of the etheric body can actually cause sensation in the physical body. There are also some green drinks and nutritional supplements that contribute to healing breaks in the etheric body.

We are complex beyond the obvious, The Bible says we are "fearfully and wonderfully made," and healing takes place on many levels so be patient with the process. One step at a time, one day at a time, is how this thing goes.

MASLOW'S HIERARCHY OF NEEDS:

Abraham Maslow studied habits of self-actualized people, and observed that they were well grounded in meeting basic needs first and then progressed step by step toward agency and enlightenment along what he calls a hierarchy of needs. This was revolutionary work in its time, because previous psychological research had been done on "abnormal" or un-actualized people.

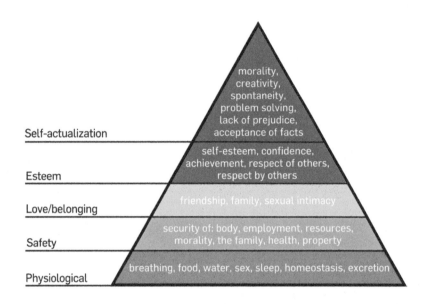

Self-actualization — morality, creativity, spontaneity, problem solving, lack of prejudice, acceptance of facts

Esteem — self-esteem, confidence, achievement, respect of others, respect by others

Love/belonging — friendship, family, sexual intimacy

Safety — security of: body, employment, resources, morality, the family, health, property

Physiological — breathing, food, water, sex, sleep, homeostasis, excretion

ERIK ERIKSON'S EIGHT AGES OF MAN: EIGHT STAGES OF PSYCHOSOCIAL DEVELOPMENT:

Psychologist Erik Erikson structures human development on an evolutionary continuum through the lifespan, moving from relative self-focus and evolving into greater altruism.

STAGE	AGES	BASIC CONFLICT	IMPORTANT EVENT	SUMMARY
1. Oral-Sensory	Birth to 12 to 18 months	Trust vs. Mistrust	Feeding	The infant must form a first loving, trusting relationship with the caregiver, or develop a sense of mistrust.
2. Muscular-Anal	18 months to 3 years	Autonomy vs. Shame/Doubt	Toilet training	The child's energies are directed toward the development of physical skills, including walking, grasping, and rectal sphincter control. The child learns control but may develop shame and doubt if not handled well.
3. Loco-motor	3 to 6 years	Initiative vs. Guilt	Independence	The child continues to become more assertive and to take more initiative, but may be too forceful, leading to guilt feelings.
4. Latency	6 to 12 years	Industry vs. Inferiority	School	The child must deal with demands to learn new skills or risk a sense of inferiority, failure and incompetence.
5. Adolescence	12 to 18 years	Identity vs. Role Confusion	Peer relationships	The teenager must achieve a sense of identity in occupation, sex roles, politics, and religion.
6. Young Adulthood	19 to 40 years	Intimacy vs. Isolation	Love relationship	The young adult must develop intimate relationships or suffer feelings of isolation.
7. Middle Adulthood	40 to 65 years	Generativity vs. Stagnation	Parenting	Each adult must find some way to satisfy and support the next generation.
8. Maturity	65 to death	Ego Integrity vs. Despair	Reflection on and acceptance of one's life	The culmination is a sense of oneself as one is and of feeling fulfilled.

KABBALAH TREE OF LIFE:

The journey of awakening the spiritual self is envisioned as a spiral energy traveling upward along a strong center core "trunk," and through engaging with different emanations or attributes of God – the *Sephirot*, toward creation and enlightenment.

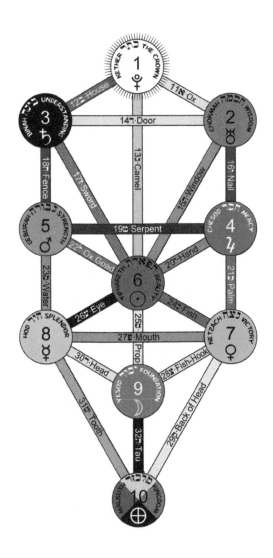

THE CHAKRA SYSTEM:

"Originating in the Hindu/yogic tradition, the Chakras are a description of the energetic body. Described as whirling energy centers of light, energy, color and vibration from the base of the spine to the third eye, along the energetic body, the Chakras correlate with many teachings that recognize the subtle or energetic body.

Jesus is teaching about this Light Body and the third eye, or pineal gland in Matthew 6:22 (in poetic language from King James Translation):

"The lamp of the body is the eye. If therefore thine eye be single, thy whole body shall be full of light. The light of the body is thine eye. If thine eye be single, thy whole body shall be full of Light."

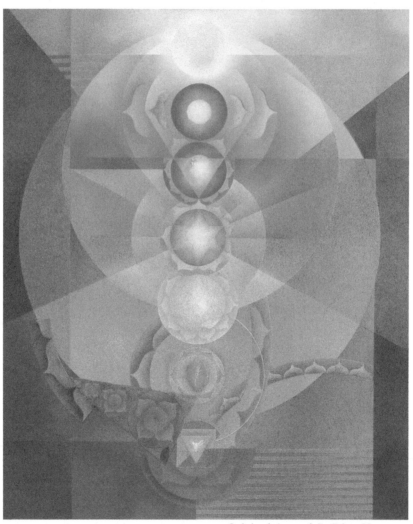

Original Artwork By Dina Hermann

CHINESE MERIDIAN SYSTEM:

Chinese medicine identifies pathways called meridians along which Chi energy flows through the body. All along the meridians are pressure points that correlate with different organs, joints and areas of the body. This is the energy highway along which acupuncture and shiatsu or acupressure heal. Both Chakras and Meridians also mirror the western scientific endocrine system.

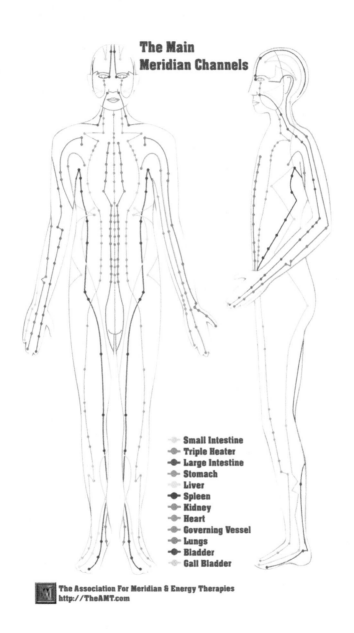

The Main Meridian Channels

- Small Intestine
- Triple Heater
- Large Intestine
- Stomach
- Liver
- Spleen
- Kidney
- Heart
- Governing Vessel
- Lungs
- Bladder
- Gall Bladder

The Association For Meridian & Energy Therapies
http://TheAMT.com

GEMSTONES:

Jasper is highly valued as a healing stone that is full of grounding energy. They can connect you deeply to the vibrations of the Earth, bringing a greater understanding of the power of nature. Jasper helps us to be less judgmental and know on a soul level that we are all connected. In some Native American culture, Jasper symbolizes the blood of the Earth, making it particularly sacred.

Carnelian is a powerful Sacral Chakra Stone. It increases personal power and physical energy, bringing you courage, compassion and a boost in creativity. Wearing or carrying Carnelian enhances vitality and will, providing you with the confidence needed to approach new projects and dreams. It is a wonderful stone to wear on a job interview, as it brings good luck and opportunity, awakening your hidden talents within. In ancient times, Egyptians buried their loved ones with Carnelian as it was thought to protect their loved ones in their journey to the afterlife and calm their fears about rebirth.

Citrine is a stone of light and happiness. It does not hold any negative energy and therefore never needs to be cleansed. It brings clarity to those who wear it and helps to manifest anything you desire to bring into your life. It activates your imagination, bringing more creative visions to a clearer mind and a more positive outlook in life. Powered by the Sun, Citrine warms, cleanses and energizes the body, energizing and strengthening the solar plexus.

Turquoise is known as the "Master Healer," and is said to be the bridge between Heaven, Sky and the Earth. Many Native American cultures believe that Turquoise helps to connect the mind to the infinite possibilities of the Universe and is considered very sacred in Chinese cultures as well. It is a Throat Chakra stone, as it helps to foster honest and open communication from the heart. It works to protect and align the chakras, strengthening the overall body in the process.

Blue Lace Agate is a wonderful stone for activating and healing the Throat Chakra. It enhances verbal communication and expression, while promoting the acceptance of your emotions. It is a very supportive stone that calms your nerves, bringing a sense of peacefulness. Blue Lace Agate is an especially helpful stone for those who may be feeling depressed or worried. It can also be used to relieve insomnia and ease tension headaches.

Lapis Lazuli is a stone that has existed since the beginning of time. It is a gemstone of total awareness that connects the wearer to a higher truth. Lapis Lazuli helps to foster verbal expression, opening and balancing the Throat Chakra. It provides wisdom and connects you to your spiritual guardians, shielding you from negative energy and returning any negative vibrations back to their source.

Rhodonite helps to balance the emotions and calm impatience. It is a very supportive stone that works with the Heart Chakra to attract love, ground negative energies and see areas in your life that can be improved upon. Rhodonite helps you to rediscover your inner gifts, bringing out much-needed love into the world. It also assists you in discovering your true passion and learning brand new skills to enhance that passion.

Amethyst is a natural stress reliever, purifier and is a crystal of spiritual growth and protection. It brings clarity of the mind to its owner and helps you to become more in tune with your feelings so that you get to know yourself on a much deeper level. Amethyst crystals repel negative energy.

Soapstone exerts a calming influence on the person using it. It is used when undergoing great changes in one's life and helps to prepare you for anything! It is thought to allow your ideas and inspirations to broaden, open and develop. It is said to open pathways between our physical plane and other planes of existence--for both sending and receiving. It allows you to give up old patterns and pathways and "go with the flow."

Selenite is the ideal crystal for all types of energy clearing. It has the ability to clear, protect and shield your energy body as well as clearing the energy of your other crystals and home. It quickly unblocks any stagnant or negative energy to create a smooth flow of positive energy. Selenite crystals magnify the energy of any other gemstone that is placed upon it, making it perfect for reactivating and recharging your jewelry and other healing crystals. It has also been recently used in holistic medicine treatments for physical healing, including cancer treatment and tumor reduction.

Combine with any stone to amplify the energy, or use alone for clarity:

Clear Quartz is a stone of manifestation that energizes and activates the energy centers within the body. It helps the wearer to think clearly, allowing them to focus and become clear about their dreams and desires. Assisting with spiritual development, Clear Quartz assists in removing blockages in the body so that energy can flow smoothly.

ALTERED STATES/ PRAYER AND MEDITATION:

Sometime in 1979, I discovered Unity teacher Eric Butterworth, who was then speaking every Sunday at Avery Fisher Hall at Lincoln Center in New York City. For one hour on Sunday mornings, I absorbed Eric's wisdom talks on metaphysics and philosophy. These Sundays opened me to the power of possibility through access to my own unconscious mind and the use of Universal Spiritual Principles.

One Sunday Eric addressed something that I had wondered about. He talked about LSD. I had experienced profound insights on LSD during college experiments but I never could actually figure out how to access or integrate those insights after the trip. Eric explained that the insights one has during a psychedelic drug experience are "real," but that once the drug is gone from the system, so is the stairway to get to the insight! He said that prayer and meditation are much more reliable ways to build the stairs or ladder to that peak insight place, so you can travel up and down without taking a trip. Cool. Better solution.

"A person with Ubuntu is open and available to others, affirming of others, does not feel threatened that others are able and good, based from a proper self-assurance that comes from knowing that he or she belongs in a greater whole and is diminished when others are humiliated or diminished.

One of the sayings in our country is Ubuntu – the essence of being human.

Ubuntu speaks particularly about the fact that you can't exist as a human being in isolation. It speaks about our interconnectedness.

You can't be human all by yourself, and when you have this quality – Ubuntu – you are known for your generosity.

We think of ourselves far too frequently as just individuals, separated from one another, whereas you are connected, and what you do affects the whole World.

When you do well, it spreads out; it is for the whole of humanity."

-DESMOND TUTU

YOU HAVE A STORY TO TELL

We are a storytelling people, we humans. Whether it is around the fire, at the virtual fire of Facebook, Instagram or Twitter, in a one-on-one conversation, in a play or book or concert, we each have something important to offer. Our gift is not fully activated until we give it away.

The laws of circulation and reciprocity require us to become a presence for healing and transformation on the planet. The only way we get across the bridge back to life and fully become part of the family of humankind, is to risk again, to jump into life, with all of its uncertainty and pain, its joy and loss and messiness.

In Matthew 25, Jesus relates a story about a final reckoning moment in which a kind of accounting of one's life is made. Heaven and hell are ways to describe inner states. This story pretty much defines the journey beyond the inner walk and into service of our fellow beings and our world.

When the Son of Man comes in his glory, and all the angels with him, then he will sit on the throne of his glory. The nations will be gathered before him, and he will separate people one from another as a shepherd separates the sheep from the goats. He will put the sheep at his right hand and the goats at the left. Then the king will say to those at his right hand, "Come, you that are blessed by my Father, inherit the kingdom prepared for you from the foundation of the world;

For I was hungry and you gave me food, I was thirsty and you gave me something to drink, I was a stranger and you welcomed me, was naked and you gave me clothing, I was sick and you took care of me, I was in prison and you visited me."

The righteous will answer him, "Lord, when was it that we saw you hungry and gave you food, or thirsty and gave you something to drink? When was it that we saw you a stranger and welcomed you, or naked and gave you clothing? When was it that we saw you sick or in prison and visited you?" The king will answer them, "Truly I tell you, just as you did it to one of the least of these you did it unto me."

That pretty much says it all. The way we pay all of this enlightenment forward is to recognize God in the people who need our kindness or mentoring or encouragement, and also in the people who hurt us or betray us or don't honor us. The life giving benefit of sharing our inner light with another is immeasurable. Start now.

Another way to say this comes from the AA Program: *"When anyone anywhere reaches out for help, I want the hand of AA always to be there, and for that I am responsible."* I think if you take out the AA reference, and replace it with "I want the hand of love always to be there..." you have a great prescription for living.

So now get going! I can't wait to hear how your journey goes. Share your genius.

Welcome home, Pass it on...

APPRECIATION

The individualistic society in which we live is one that does not value human life as much as it honors progress and technical pyrotechnics. We have lost so much in our pursuit of transitory success. And one of the greatest losses is that we have ceased to honor the elders. The elders are the wisdom holders. We lose touch with them at the peril of our world. There is no way I can adequately thank the Universe for sending me my teacher, Rev. Dr. Cecil Murray. I recognized in him the soul of the ages, and have shared the deepest longings of my heart with him. He has always been there for me, challenging me, encouraging my deeper journey, defending me, making me laugh (mostly at myself), and teaching me every day.

You will find your teacher if you allow yourself to be teachable. Stay open at the top, and allow inspiration to order your steps.

Thank you Pastor Murray. Bless you.

Afterword:

An article in the March 2015 issue of Atlantic Monthly churned up 12-Step communities, social media and some mainstream news arteries like National Public Radio. The article makes a good point about the 12-Steps being used in the majority of professional treatment programs as the basic treatment model when the science of addiction study is available. This is true. AA is NOT a scientifically based program, never pretended to be! It is a psycho-spiritual path and a totally amazing, channeled tool for Recovery 1.0. But beyond that beginning stage it is true that many recovering people get stuck if they don't keep growing.

By this I mean that recovering people need to learn about the physiological effects of drugs and alcohol, patterns of self-induced drug states through process addictions like food, sex, shopping etc, and then learn some communication skills. Then to really make progress get some Gestalt therapy!! So the author makes a great point. And the irony is that if the medical model really worked to create lasting sobriety on its own, the treated person may never need to go to AA. But the medical model hasn't proved to be effective without the addition of the 12-Steps in too many cases, so the combination of the two seems to be the best way to go.

The 12-Steps are an authentic spiritual path, and one that works for life. Because a balanced life includes Body, Mind and Spirit healing, there is really no conflict here.

The GREAT thing about the 12-Steps is that they work by ATTRACTION AND NOT PROMOTION. So where the not good part comes in is that you can't SENTENCE someone to sobriety. It is a gift of grace. If treatment programs knew how to bottle the miracle of AA, they wouldn't have to use meetings as the basis of their suggestions for maintenance! Treatment programs that are living on insurance payments drag their whole caseload to public AA meetings, and why? Because AA works!! So the REAL gift for me was entering an intensive Alcohol and Drug Studies certificate program at Cypress College...Yes, I was able to then work in what we laughably call "the field" when I graduated, but really? I understood myself so much better through these studies! And THAT is what liberates.

For first level recovery: 12-Step Meetings

And honestly, insurance should not be paying for private programs to take vans full of people to a free, voluntary psycho-spiritual program.

For second stage recovery, science based learning: School

Education is power! Check out a two year college somewhere and LEARN about yourself!!! What a great gift! THAT is where you will learn science based recovery information that will blow your mind for real!!

For a spiritual path: The Gateways
You hold them in your hand.

ACKNOWLEDGMENTS

The process of giving birth to this book was one I never dreamed would be so challenging. I am deeply grateful to *Gleah Powers* for challenging me to clarify in writing what works for me, and to make something practical for people to use.

Caraid O'Brien is simply a genius and not only read drafts along the way, but lovingly pointed out that I had three books in my first draft. One is now a one woman performance piece, one is a book on Jesus, and this is the book I thought I was writing all along. Thank you so much Caraid.

Rev. Dr. Robert Brashear has read and really wrestled with me about the text, about the theology that was emerging, and pointed out places where he wanted more information. Honestly Bob, I cannot thank you enough.

And of course, *Dr. Cecil Murray*, my father in the ministry, friend, mentor and defender has read at least six versions of the entire text, and his clarity and brilliance helped me to have confidence in what was emerging through me. Thank you so very much for "propping me up on every leaning side" Pastor...always.

Mike Patchett, you have never ceased to believe in me and even in the darkest hours have seen the Light, and reminded me about what is really important. My gratitude for you is boundless.

Thank you so much to my amazing friends, who have read drafts, and helped with critical insights along the way.

Sally Sockwell, who always hears what I am trying to say, helps me say it better, inspires me with her own astonishing work, and who appreciates my crafts.

Walter Bobbie who is a brilliant actor, Tony Award winning Director, a writer, painter, amazing man who makes me LAUGH harder than any human...often at myself, thank God. Thank you Walter for cutting to the chase, discovering the first sentence on the fortieth page, and for giving me a third chance to be on time for the theatre.

Deborah Love, *Judith Loniak*, long-time sisters on the journey, your notes were like breadcrumbs along the path as I worked to find what did and didn't belong in the book.

And thank you too to *Jeffrey Lepinske*, for constant and delightful friendship of the Spirit, for being a co-conspirator in noticing beautiful things even in the midst of chaos, and for being by my side…my angel actually, from Day One of a life transforming journey.

Norbert Norman and *Eduardo Vanzini*, thank you both, for "getting it" – all of it. You each have breathed life, art, resources of many kinds; style, brilliance, friendship into the dream of a multi-dimensional spiritual expression that was insisting to emerge through me. Norbert, you brought us the Mayan elders, a million ways to order lunch at Le Pain Quotidian, and so much more. Thank you both for sharing your spiritual journeys and friendship with me, I am a blessed woman.

Karen Osit, you will never know really how grateful I am to you. You saw just me, at a time when I was somehow learning about being a projection screen for things I didn't really understand. In the middle of all that, we forged a friendship, and that made enough room in me to keep going. Thank you, thank you, bless you. There is no one with whom I would rather go to the theatre, take a lazy drive along the Hudson, or wrestle to understand a totally different way of seeing the world.

Eleni Yalanis…You must know how grateful I am for you sharing your journey with me. As I began writing this book, you were in my life in one rather formal role, and over the years have become a spiritual little sister (and wise elder too), have miraculously made the world of the website stay alive even when I wasn't sure I was going to, and so much more. Thank you so much for all of the ways you enrich my journey.

Caitlin Crest, thank you for getting at the heart of this material as editor, designer, midwife.

And to my *Leadership Long Beach Class of 2015*- The Perfect Class- You will never know how grateful I am for you literally having my back during one of the most challenging years of my life to date!! You would not let me go backward. You inspire me every day. Thank you from the bottom of my heart.

I also thank my entire *Sanctuary NYC community*. This idea was coming forth for the two years we were meeting together as our Beloved Community in New York City, on 86th St, and your talent, love, enthusiasm and friendship midwifed this baby into being. Bless you…all of you.

A very specific thank you goes to the *Ministry Team*, with whom I had the honor of meeting every Tuesday evening for three years! We all learned so much, mentored one another, and incubated the next stages of our work in that matrix. Nancy Napier, Carol Napier, Jeffrey

Lepinske, Michelle Ruiz, thank you. And thank you too Nancy, for shoving me at this work. You know what I mean by this. Thank you.

And finally I thank every person who has shared your journey into these 12-Steps and your deeper spiritual journey with me. Your courage, tenacity, humor and bravery continue to inspire and humble me.

Jane

{you and God are one}

SOURCES AND RESOURCES

Books:

Chilton, Bruce (2000) *Rabbi Jesus: An Intimate Biography - The Jewish Life and Teaching That Inspired Christianity pgs. 12-13.* Random House, N.Y.

Miles, Jack and Doniger, Wendy (Eds.). (2014). *The Norton Anthology of World Religions Volumes 1 and 2.* W. W. Norton and Company, NY, NY

James, W. (2013). *Varieties of Religious Experience.* CreateSpace Publishing

Allen, J. (2011). *As A Man Thinketh.* Tribeca Books, NYC

Klotz, N.D. (2005). *Original Prayer: Teachings and Meditations on the Aramaic Words of Jesus.* Audio CD, Sounds True, Incorporated

Alcoholics Anonymous (1976). (3rd ed.). Alcoholics Anonymous World Services NYC

Dr. Bob and the Good Old-Timers (1980). Alcoholics Anonymous World Services

Maltz, M. (1989). *Psycho-Cybernetics-A New Way to Get More Living Out of Life.* Pocket Books NY

Maslow, A. (2011). *Toward a Psychology of Being.* Martino Fine Books, Eastford, CT

Erikson, E. H. (1993). *Childhood and Society.* W.W. Norton and Company

Holmes, E. (2010). *The Science of Mind.* Tarcher, NY

Fox, E. (2009). *The Sermon on the Mount; The Key to Success in Life.* Harper One

Wa'Na'Nee'Che (1993). (Renault, Dennis and Freke,Timothy), Native American Spirituality, HarperCollins, NY

Meyer, M. (Ed.). (2009). , *The Nag Hammadi Scriptures -The Revised and Updated Translation of Sacred Gnostic Texts,* Harper One

Meeks, W. A. (Ed.). (1993). *HarperCollins Study Bible: New Revised Standard Version.* Harper One

Greene, J. M. (2009). *Gita Wisdom: An Introduction to India's Essential Yoga Text.* Mandala Publishing, CA

Films:

Century of the Self-Film. (2002). Produced by Curtis, K. and Lambert, A. Directed by Lambert, A.

What The Bleep Do We Know? (2005). Chasse, Vincente and Arntz (Directors)

CPSIA information can be obtained
at www.ICGtesting.com
Printed in the USA
BVOW05s1823270417

482529BV00015B/103/P